Soccer: The 6-Week Plan

The contents of this book were carefully researched. However, all information is supplied without liability. Neither the author nor the publisher will be liable for possible disadvantages or damages resulting from this book.

TOTO SCHMUGGE

SOCCER:
THE 6-WEEK PLAN

THE GUIDE TO BUILDING A
SUCCESSFUL TEAM

Meyer & Meyer Sport

British Library Cataloguing in Publication Data

A catalogue record for this book is available from the British Library.

Soccer: The 6-Week Plan

Maidenhead: Meyer & Meyer Sport (UK) Ltd., 2016

ISBN: 978-1-78255-092-1

© 2016 by Meyer & Meyer Sport (UK) Ltd.

Aachen, Auckland, Beirut, Cairo, Cape Town, Dubai, Hägendorf, Hong Kong,

Indianapolis, Manila, New Delhi, Singapore, Sydney, Tehran, Vienna

Member of the World Sport Publishers' Association (WSPA)

Manufacturing: Print Consult GmbH, Munich, Germany

ISBN: 978-1-78255-092-1

E-Mail: info@m-m-sports.com

www.m-m-sports.com

CONTENTS

 ## WEEK 1, DAY 1

Warm-Up

Exercise 1: Enter and Coordination (10 minutes)

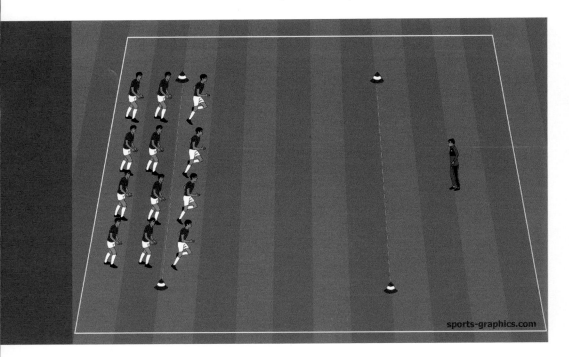

sports-graphics.com

Setup
○ Mark start and finish lines at a distance of 33 feet.
○ Divide players into four groups to avoid long waiting times.

Sequence
○ Butt kicks
○ High knee skips
○ Side-steps forward
○ Side-steps backward
○ Lateral running (turn the body and move the legs)
○ High knee skips
○ Run backwards
○ Jump-run forward
○ Forward side left/jumping
○ High jumps
○ Run in place
○ Sprint to the finish line

Soccer: The 6-Week Plan

Exercise 2: Ball Habituation and Passing Game (10 minutes)

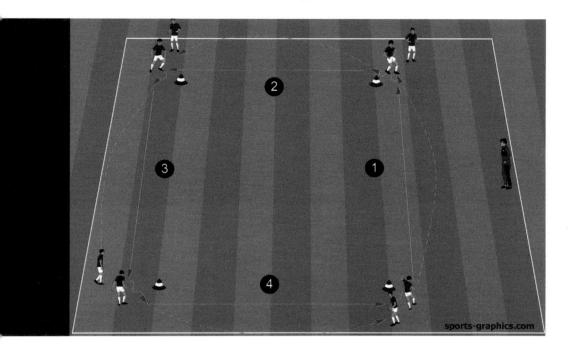

Setup
○ Use cones to mark out a square 33 feet by 33 feet. Create as many squares as necessary for the number of players.
○ Each cone has two players.
○ Each group has one ball.

Sequence
○ Player 1 passes the ball to player 2, then follows the ball to the second cone.
○ Player 2 takes the ball with a touch to the side and passes to player 3, then follows the ball to the third cone, and so on.

Tips
○ Pay attention to detail; make sure the players are concentrating when performing the exercises.
○ With a defeat (a bad first touch or if the player needs more than two touches), the whole group must do 10 push-ups.

Main Exercise: 5-v-2 Corner Play (25 minutes)

Setup

O   Use cones to mark out a square 33 feet by 33 feet. Create as many squares as necessary for the number of players.

O   Each field has seven players, with the two youngest players in the middle.

Sequence

O   The outer players adapt to any position of the ball.

O   The two players in the middle try to win the ball.

O   The player who loses the ball must be in the middle.

O   When there are more than 20 ball touches without players in the middle getting the ball, the players in the middle stay in the middle for double the time.

Conclusion: Old Versus Young (2x20 minutes)

Setup

O   Use cones to mark out a playing field that goes from penalty area to penalty area and place a goal at each end of the field.

O   Divide players into two teams based on their ages (i.e., an older team and a younger team).

Sequence

O   Play without offside.

O   A goal only counts if all players from the attacking team are in the opposing half of the field.

O   All players from the defending team must be in their own half, otherwise the goal counts double.

WEEK 1, DAY 2

Warm-Up: Force and Stabilization Program (15 minutes)

Exercise 1: Push-Ups

O   Do 30 reps.

Exercise 2: Sit-Ups

O   Do 30 reps.

Exercise 3: Alternating Plank (20 reps)

O   Assume the plank position and alternate slowly lifting the right and left legs.

O   Do 20 reps.

Exercise 4: Side Plank

O   Assume a side plank position and then raise and lower the top leg.

O   Do 15 reps per side.

Exercise 5

O   While lying face down with the feet flexed and toes firmly on the ground, put the
    hands in the air behind the body and then swing them to the front.

O   Do 20 reps.

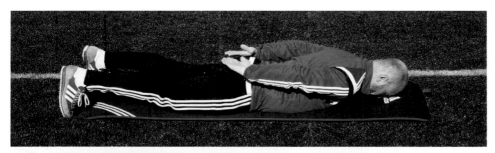

Exercise 6

○   Using the forearm and heel for support, lift the body slightly off the ground.

○   While keeping the body in the air, extend the other leg.

○   Hold each leg for 15-20 seconds.

Exercise 7

○   Start in a forearm plank position.

○   Lift the opposite hand and leg and hold for 10-20 seconds.

○   Repeat with the other hand and leg.

Conclusion: Tournament Form, Small Box, 4-v-4 Game (35 minutes)

Setup

O   Make a field that is twice the size of the penalty area.

O   Split players into four teams (depending on the number of players).

Sequence

O   Teams play a free, 4-v-4 game.

O   Each team plays each other twice (first and second round).

O   Winner of the tournament is the team that finishes with the most wins.

O   The team that is in last place must clean up the playing/training field.

Main Exercise 1: 4x4-Minute Runs (30 minutes)

Setup

O   Put one cone at each corner of the penalty area.

Sequence

O   Players run around the cones for 4 minutes followed by a 3-minute break.

O   Repeat for a total of four runs.

O   If a lactate test was performed, players should run at 85-90% of the maximum pulse.

O   If there are no values, each player should run about 70-80% of maximum speed BBs.

Main Exercise 2: Ball Acclimatization Passing Game (10 minutes)

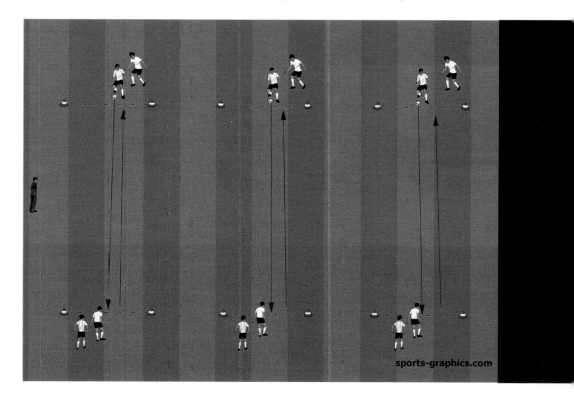

sports-graphics.com

Setup

O   Make several pairs of 5-foot goals approximately 32 feet apart, depending on the level of performance.

O   Put 2-3 players at every goal.

O   Each pair of goals gets one ball.

Sequence

O   Player passes the ball through the goals and then switches places with his or her teammate.

O   After the opposite player receives the pass, the ball is returned through the other goal.

O   Players continue to pass the ball back and forth through the goals.

WEEK 1, DAY 3

Warm-Up 1: Running and Power Circuit (40 minutes)

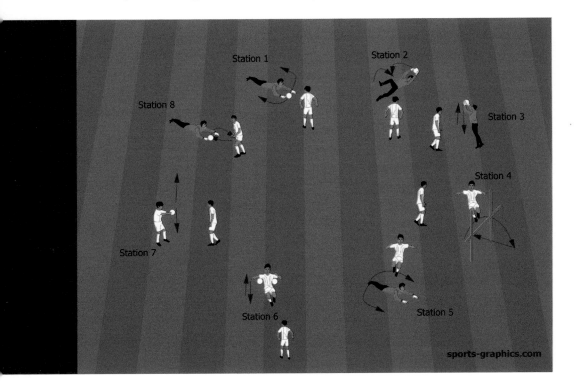

Setup

O   Create a power circuit with eight stations. Place a medicine ball (4-10 lbs depending on the level of performance) at seven of the stations and a hurdle at station 4.

O   Two players work together at each station.

Sequence

O **Station 1:** While lying on the stomach with the legs slightly lifted off the ground, hold the medicine ball out in front and roll sideways back and forth. The legs and the medicine ball may not touch the ground.

O **Station 2:** Lie on the back holding the medicine ball back with the upper body. Keeping the arms extended, lift one leg and stretch to the medicine ball. Repeat, alternating legs.

O **Station 3:** Jump while holding the medicine ball above the head.

O **Station 4:** Side jump back and forth over the hurdle, alternating the lead foot each time.

O **Station 5:** One partner lies on his or her stomach, and the other partner jumps or skips side to side over him or her.

O **Station 6:** Hold two medicine balls and jump, bringing the knees up as high as possible.

O **Station 7:** Hold the medicine ball with straight arms in front of your body. Throw the ball straight up, then quickly lie down on the ground and get back up, catching the ball before it hits the ground.

O **Station 8:** One player begins the exercise lying on the stomach. The partner throws the medicine ball to him or her and then lies down on the ground. The first partner immediately gets up without the ball touching the ground, and the exercise repeats.

Tips

O The partners take turns at each station.

O Perform the exercises at high speed so players can get the most out of the workout.

O The exercises should be performed in about 20-40 seconds (depending on the power level) per play.

Warm-Up 2: Ball-Passing Game (10 minutes)

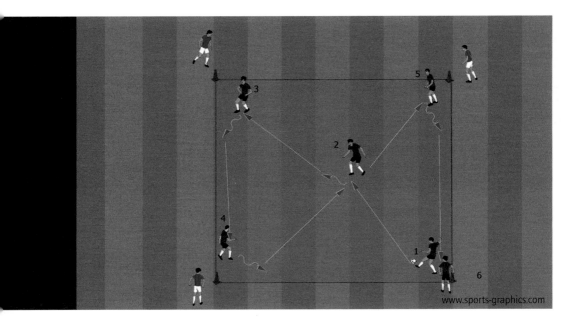

Setup
○   Use four cones to mark off an area about 20 x 33 feet.

○   Two players begin at each cone, with one player in the center.

Sequence
○   Player 1 passes the ball to player 2 (in the middle), calls "Turn!" and follows the ball.

○   Player 2 turns with a ball touch to the other side, passes to player 3, calls "Turn!" and follows the ball.

○   Player 3 takes the ball with a touch to the side, passes to player 4, calls "Turn!" and follows the ball.

○   Player 4 takes the ball with a touch to the front, passes to player 1 (now standing in the middle), calls "Turn!" and follows the ball to the middle.

○   Player 1 turns with a ball touch to the other side, passes to player 5, calls "Turn!" and and follows the ball.

○   Player 5 takes the ball with a touch to the side and play continues to player 6, and so on.

Main Exercise: Fast Switch (2x10 minutes)

www.sports-graphics.com

Setup

O   Use cones to mark a playing field about 130 feet in length and 18 yards wide with a goal at each end.

O   Divide players into two teams.

O   The coach stands with a supply of balls on the sideline.

Sequence

O   The two teams play against each other.

O   The defending team defends both goals and the other team can score in both goals.

O   When the ball is won by the defending team, they must try to keep the ball as long as possible.

O   When the attacking team scores a goal, a new ball for the defending team is played into the game immediately from the outside, then the attacking team gets the ball.

O   After 10 minutes, switch the teams so that the defenders become the attackers and the attackers become the defenders.

O   The team that scores the most goals wins the game.

Conclusion: Final 11-v-11 Game (10 minutes)

sports-graphics.com

Setup
○ Mark the playing field from penalty area to penalty area with a goal at each end.
○ Divide players into older and younger teams.

Sequence
○ Play without offsides.
○ Goals only count if all players of the attacking team are in the opposing half.
○ All players from the defending team must be on their half, otherwise the goal counts double.

WEEK 1, DAY 4

Warm-Up Cycle

www.sports-graphics.com

Setup
- ○ Make an outer track by placing cones on the penalty corners.
- ○ In the interior of the outer course, build a second course with obstacles:
    - ○ A series of hurdles approximately 16 feet apart
    - ○ Poles
    - ○ Two sticks laid end to end

Sequence
- ○ Each player runs at speed of 90% of the maximum pulse rate.
- ○ Players run around the outer track and then move to the inner obstacle course.
- ○ Jump over the hurdles, run through the poles, and hop back and forth over the sticks, using one bar to hop on the left foot and the other to hop on the right foot.
- ○ Continue to repeat the outer and inner courses for 4 minutes.
- ○ Players should do a total of four 4-minute sessions with a 3-minute break between each.

1

Warm-Up With Ball: Passing Game (10 minutes)

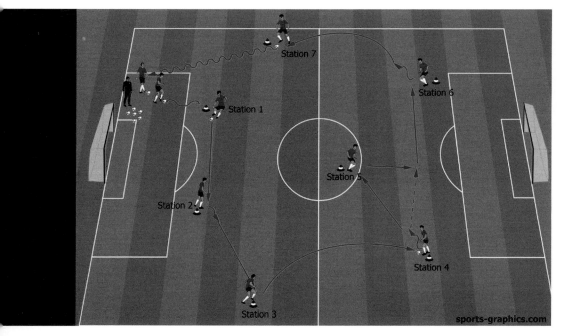

Setup

- Set up seven cones approximately 32-50 feet apart.
- Place two or three players at each cone.

Sequence

- Player 1 passes to player 2 and calls out "Turn!"
- Player 2 takes the ball with a touch in the lane, passes it to player 3, and calls out "Turn!"
- Player 3 takes the ball with a contact in the lane, plays a long ball flight to player 4, and calls out "Turn!"
- Player 4 takes the ball out of the air with a contact in the course, passes to player 5, and calls out "Turn!"
- Player 5 kicks the ball back to player 4.
- Player 4 kicks the ball to player 6 and calls out "Turn!"
- Player 6 takes the ball with a contact to the side, plays a long flight ball to player 7, and calls out "Turn!"
- Player 7 takes the ball out of the air with a contact in the barrel and dribbles to the start cone.

Main Exercise: Game Shape 6-6-6 (30 minutes)

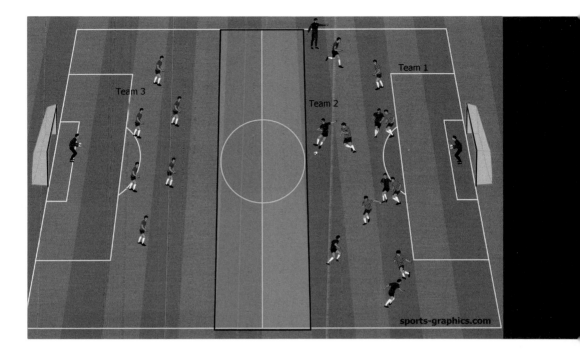

Setup
- ○ Create three fields using cones placed 32 feet on either side of the center line.
- ○ Divide players into 3 teams.
- ○ Both goals are on the baseline with a goalkeeper in each goal.

Sequence
- ○ Whichever team is in a field with a goal must defend that goal.
- ○ Team 2 attacks and tries to score a goal against team 1 while team 3 has the first break time.
- ○ If team 1 wins the ball, they must try to dribble the ball into the middle zone while team 2 tries to prevent this.
- ○ If team 1 manages to dribble the ball into the middle zone, they start the attack in the next zone, where team 3 defends the other goal.
- ○ Team 2 has a break along the way and then must defend in the next attack, and so on.

1

Conclusion: End Game (10 minutes)

Setup
O   Make the playing field from penalty area to penalty area with a goal on each end line.
O   Divide players into two teams.

Sequence
O   The two teams play a free game with offsides.
O   The losing team must clear up the space.

WEEK 2, DAY 5

Warm-Up: Force and Stabilization Program (20 minutes)

O   Each station has two or three players.

O   Players take a 20-30-second break between each station.

O   After one round, players take a 3-minute break.

O   Repeat for a second round.

Exercise 1: Push-Ups

O   Repeat for 20-30 seconds.

Exercise 2: Sit-Ups

O   Repeat for 20-30 seconds.

Exercise 3: Alternating Plank (20 reps)

O   Assume the plank position and alternate slowly lifting the right and left legs.

O   Repeat for 20-30 seconds.

Exercise 4: Side Plank

○   Assume a side plank position and then raise and lower the top leg.

○   Repeat for 20-30 seconds.

Exercise 5

- ◯ While lying face down with the feet flexed and toes firmly on the ground, put the hands in the air behind the body and then swing them to the front.
- ◯ Repeat for 20-30 seconds.

2

Exercise 6

○ Using the forearm and heel for support, lift the body slightly off the ground.

○ While keeping the body in the air, extend the other leg.

○ Repeat for 20-30 seconds.

Exercise 7

○ Start in a forearm plank position.

○ Lift the opposite hand and leg and hold for 20-30 seconds.

○ Repeat with the other hand and leg.

Main Exercise: Agility and Condition Course (30 minutes)

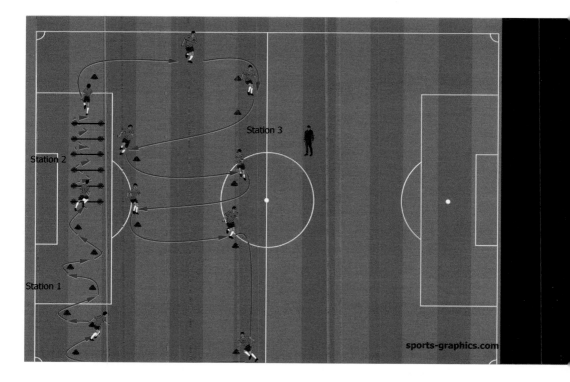

Setup

- ○ **Station 1:** Place six cones diagonally from each other.
- ○ **Station 2:** Put four hurdles with 16 feet between each hurdle.
- ○ **Station 3:** Place six cones in a zig-zag formation with 33 feet in between each cone.

Main Exercise: Coordination and Technique (10 minutes)

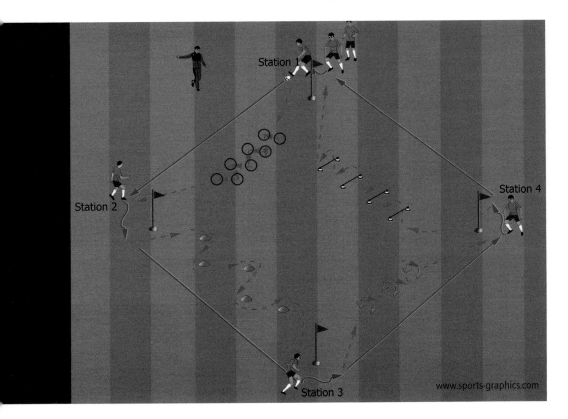

Setup

O   Use four cones to create a 33-by-33-foot square.

O   Between each cone put the stations:

   O   **Station 1:** Set up six rings.

   O   **Station 2:** Set up five cones in the zig-zag formation.

   O   **Station 3:** Set up three hurdles.

   O   **Station 4:** Place five poles in a row 20 inches apart.

O   Put two or three players on each cone.

Sequence

O Player 1 passes the ball to player 2 and runs through the ring course (with a step in each ring), then goes to the next cone.

O Player 2 takes the ball with a touch to the side, passes to player 3, and runs through the cones course with quick steps

O Player 3 takes the ball with a touch to the side, passes to player 4, and jumps over the three hurdles.

O Player 4 takes the ball with a touch to the side and passes to the next player who goes hopping through the bars.

O Repeat 3 times, 10 minutes with 2 minute breaks.

2

Conclusion: 6-v-6 Tournament Form Game

sports-graphics.com

Setup

O   Mark out a field 180 by 82 feet with two large goals at each end.

O   Divide players into teams of six.

Sequence

O   Play six 2-minute tournament games.

O   The champion is the team with the most wins.

O   The losing team must pick up the cones from the field.

WEEK 2, DAY 6

Warm-Up: Force and Stabilization Program (20 minutes)

○ Each station has two or three players.

○ Players take a 20-30-second break between each station.

○ After one round, players take a 3-minute break.

○ Repeat for a second round.

Exercise 1: Push-Ups

○ Repeat for 20-30 seconds.

Exercise 2: Sit-Ups

○ Repeat for 20-30 seconds.

Exercise 3: Alternating Plank (20 reps)

O   Assume the plank position and alternate slowly lifting the right and left legs.

O   Repeat for 20-30 seconds.

Exercise 4: Side Plank

O   Assume a side plank position and then raise and lower the top leg.

O   Repeat for 20-30 seconds.

Exercise 5

○   While lying face down with the feet flexed and toes firmly on the ground, put the
    hands in the air behind the body and then swing them to the front.

○   Repeat for 20-30 seconds.

Exercise 6

○   Using the forearm and heel for support, lift the body slightly off the ground.

○   While keeping the body in the air, extend the other leg.

○   Repeat for 20-30 seconds.

Exercise 7

○   Start in a forearm plank position.

○   Lift the opposite hand and leg and hold for 20-30 seconds.

○   Repeat with the other hand and leg.

Main Exercise: Tempo Runs (15 minutes)

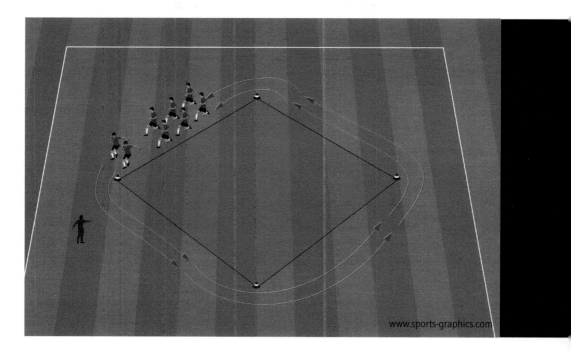

www.sports-graphics.com

Setup:

O   Use four cones to mark a 50-by-50-foot square.

O   Line players up in two rows.

O   Build as many courses as necessary to accommodate the number of players and keep wait times minimal.

Sequence

O   The players run in two lines at a slow pace to the first cone.

O   At the cone, the first two players increase their pace until they catch up with the end of the lines.

O   After those first players have run at a high pace for a distance of one and a half sides of the square, the next two players increase their pace until they catch up with the end of the line.

O   This continues until each player has run at a high pace five times.

Main Exercise: Technique Exercises (15 minutes)

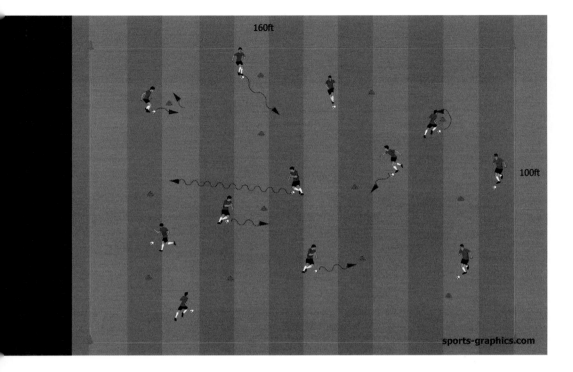

Setup

○   Use four cones to mark off a 160-by-100-foot field.

○   Distribute 14 cones throughout the field.

○   Give each player a ball.

Sequence

○   All players perform specific tricks during the dribbling before a cone (e.g., step over, screwing, lunge, soles trick, Beckenbauer rotation, Zidane trick, and so on).

○   Everything should be done at the highest pace possible in order to provoke chaos in the field!

Main Exercise: Keep Ball (20 minutes)

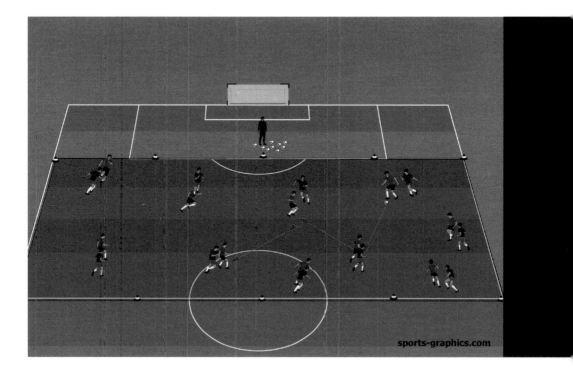

sports-graphics.com

Setup

O Mark out a field from the penalty area up to the midline. This field should have no goals.

O Divide players into two teams.

Sequence

O Play two 8-minute free games.

O After seven passes without an opponent getting the ball, the team with the ball receives a point.

O The team that has more points at the end wins.

Conclusion: 6-v-6 End Game With Time Limit (20 minutes)

Setup

○ Use four cones to mark a 200-by-52-foot playing field with a goal at each end.

○ Divide players into three teams of six players (or whatever best suits the number of players).

Sequence

○ Each team plays the others twice for 4 minutes at a time.

○ The attacking team has only 5 seconds to play the ball from their half into the opposing half.

○ There is no time limit while a team is in the opposing half.

WEEK 2, DAY 7

Warm-Up: Running and Power Circuit (40 minutes)

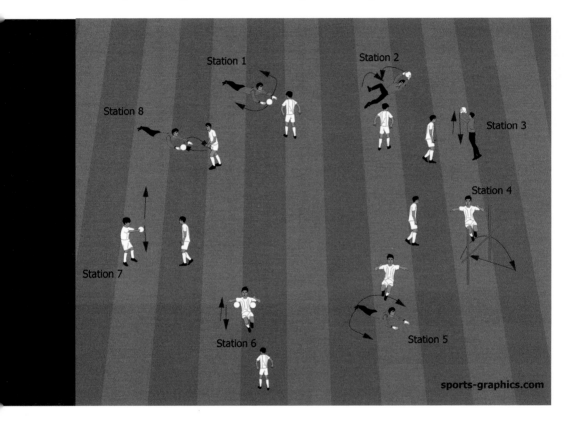

Setup

O Create a power circuit with eight stations. Place a medicine ball (4-10 lbs depending on the level of performance) at seven of the stations and a hurdle at station 4.

O Two players work together at each station.

Sequence

○ **Station 1:** While lying on the stomach with the legs slightly lifted off the ground, hold the medicine ball out in front and roll sideways back and forth. The legs and the medicine ball may not touch the ground.

○ **Station 2:** Lie on the back holding the medicine ball back with the upper body. Keeping the arms extended, lift one leg and stretch to the medicine ball. Repeat, alternating legs.

○ **Station 3:** Jump while holding the medicine ball above the head.

○ **Station 4:** Side jump back and forth over the hurdle, alternating the lead foot each time.

○ **Station 5:** One partner lies on his or her stomach, and the other partner jumps or skips side to side over him or her.

○ **Station 6:** Hold two medicine balls and jump, bringing the knees up as high as possible.

○ **Station 7:** Hold the medicine ball with straight arms in front of your body. Throw the ball straight up, then quickly lie down on the ground and get back up, catching the ball before it hits the ground.

○ **Station 8:** One player begins the exercise lying on the stomach. The partner throws the medicine ball to him or her and then lies down on the ground. The first partner immediately gets up without the ball touching the ground, and the exercise repeats.

Tips

○ The partners take turns at each station.

○ Perform the exercises at high speed so players can get the most out of the workout.

○ The exercises should be performed in about 20-40 seconds (depending on the power level) per play.

2

Main Exercise: Skill Course (10 minutes)

Setup

O   Build two obstacle courses as shown in the figure.

O   Divide players into two groups; each group has one ball.

Sequence

O   Player 1 passes to player 2 and calls out "Turn!"

O   Player 2 takes the ball with a touch to the other side and passes to player 3.

O   Player 3 takes the ball in the barrel and dribbles around the poles.

O   After the last pole, player 3 plays the ball into the goal.

O   Players should continue the pattern for 4 minutes. Which group scored the most goals in the time alotted?

O   Repeat the activity for another 4 minutes. Which group scored more goals this time?

Main Exercise: Complex 4-v-4 Game (20 minutes)

sports-graphics.com

Setup

O   Mark out two 48-by-48-foot fields, depending on the number of players.

O   Divide players into teams of four.

O   Two players from each team play inside the field, and the other two players from each team play outside of the box.

Sequence

O   A team gets a point if the ball can reach the teammates on the other side.

O   After 5 plays without the ball touching the opponent's in the field, the team gets an additional point

O   Teams will play six 3-minute games and then switch positions and opponents.

O   The team with the most wins after the tournament is the winner!

Conclusion: End Game (20 minutes)

Setup

○   Use cones to mark out a playing field between the penalty areas with a goal at each
    end.
○   Divide players into two teams.

Sequence

○   Teams play a free game with offside.
○   The losing team must clean up the practice space.

WEEK 3, DAY 8

Warm-Up 1: Strength and Stability Circuit (20 minutes)

O   Each station has two or three players.

O   Players take a 20-30-second break between each station.

O   After one round, players take a 3-minute break.

O   Repeat for a second round.

Exercise 1: Push-Ups

O   Repeat for 20-30 seconds.

Exercise 2: Sit-Ups

O   Repeat for 20-30 seconds.

Exercise 3: Alternating Plank (20 reps)

O   Assume the plank position and alternate slowly lifting the right and left legs.

O   Repeat for 20-30 seconds.

3

Exercise 4: Side Plank

O   Assume a side plank position and then raise and lower the top leg.

O   Repeat for 20-30 seconds.

Exercise 5:

○ While lying face down with the feet flexed and toes firmly on the ground, put the hands in the air behind the body and then swing them to the front.

○ Repeat for 20-30 seconds.

3

Exercise 6:

- ○   Using the forearm and heel for support, lift the body slightly off the ground.
- ○   While keeping the body in the air, extend the other leg.
- ○   Repeat for 20-30 seconds.

Exercise 7:

- ○   Start in a forearm plank position.
- ○   Lift the opposite hand and leg and hold for 20-30 seconds.
- ○   Repeat with the other hand and leg.

Warm-Up 2: Coordination Exercise 1 (10 minutes)

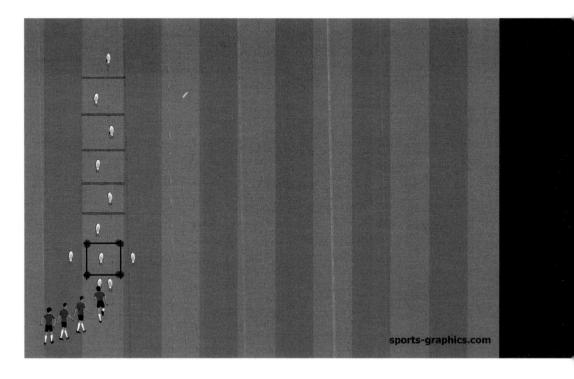

Setup

○   Set up a side-by-side coordination course with a square and five bars.

○   Split players into two groups.

Sequence

○   Take one step forward, then one step backward.

○   Take one step to the left and then one step to the right.

○   Step forward over the five bars.

○   Repeat three times.

Warm-Up 3: Coordination Exercise 2 (10 minutes)

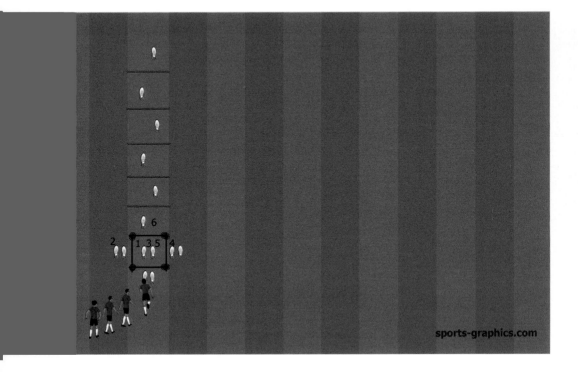

sports-graphics.com

Setup
O   Set up a side-by-side coordination course with a square and five bars.
O   Split players into two groups.

Sequence
O   Take two steps forward, then two steps backward.
O   Take two steps to the left and then two steps to the right.
O   Step forward over the five bars.
O   Repeat three times.

Warm-Up 4: Coordination Side-Steps

sports-graphics.com

Setup

O   Set up a side-by-side coordination course with a square and five bars.

O   Split players into two groups.

Sequence

O   Take one step forward, then one step backward.

O   Take one step to the left and then one step to the right.

O   Side step over the five bars.

O   Repeat four times.

Main Exercise: Back Four and 4-v-2 (10 minutes)

Setup

Group 1: Back Four

O   Split the back four to their positions.

O   Assign three players to the offense.

Group 2: 4-v-2

O   Use cones to mark out two 33-by-33-foot squares.

O   Divide the players into teams of four and teams of two.

Sequence

Group 1: Back Four

○   Teach the move of the last four using an example:

○   Player 1 passes to player 2.

○   The back four shift in a block to the ball side.

○   The fullback attacks player 2.

○   The other defensive players move and cover from the back.

○   Go through different sequences of players 1, 2, and 3 without an attack on the back four to form. This exercise is about learning the block move.

○   All defensive players are practicing, so do not forget to rotate the two groups.

Group 2: 4-v-2

○   Play four against two. Try to hold the ball.

3

Main Exercise: Back Four Long and Cross Balls and Shooting on Goal
(10 minutes)

Setup

Group 1: Back Four Long and Cross Balls

O   Split the back four to their positions.

O   Assign two players to the offense.

O   One player passes the balls in from the center line.

Group 2: Shooting on Goal

O   Put a player in the center and one on the outside.

O   The attackers are placed in front of the goal.

Sequence

Group 1: Back Four Long and Cross Balls

O   Player 1 plays a high ball to the attacker from various positions.

O   While the ball is being passed, players 5 and 3 drop back 16 feet.

O   Player 4 goes up to head the ball.

O   After 5-6 minutes, the players rotate.

Group 2: Shooting on Goal

O   Pass a high ball from the center to the starting players on the side.

O   From the outside, cross the balls.

O   Shortly before crossing the attacker, try to get the crossing ball and shoot a goal.

O   The player who played the ball to the outside moves up and has the ball when it comes back to the 18-yard box.

3

Main Exercise: Back Four 6-v-4 Game and Shooting on Goal (20 minutes)

Setup

Group 1: Back Four 6-v-4 Game

O   Divide players into two teams.

O   Put four players back on defense and six players attacking on offense.

Group 2: Shooting on Goal

O   Each player has a ball.

O   A player or coach is on the 18-yard box and passes the ball to the incoming players on the right or left sides.

Sequence

Group 1: Back Four 6-v-4 Game

O   Six offensive players play against the back four on half of the field.

O   The back four must be compact and move together.

O   Rotate players so that each player has a chance to play in his or her position.

O   When the back four win the ball, use a long ball to pass to the coach.

Group 2: Shooting on Goal

O   Player 1 passes to the player in front the 18-yard box who touches the ball to the right or left side.

O   The player who passes the ball follows and shoots on goal.

Soccer: The 6-Week Plan

Main Exercise: 6-v-5 Game With Focus on the Back Four (20 minutes)

Setup
○   Divide players into one team of five defenders and one team of six offensive players.
○   Use cones to mark two goals 19 feet apart on the midline.

Sequence
○   Play a free game without touch limitations.
○   Offensive players try to score in the regular goal.
○   When the defensive side wins the ball, they quickly try to score in the two cone goals.

Conclusion: Game (15 minutes)

Setup

○   Mark the field from 18-yard box to 18-yard box with a goal on each side.

○   Divide players into two teams.

Sequence

○   Play a free game without a touch limitation and with offside.

○   The losing team cleans the soccer field and picks up the cones.

3

WEEK 3, DAY 9

Warm-Up 1: Short Running Warm-Up (5-7 minutes)

Warm-Up 2: Pyramid Run (30 minutes)

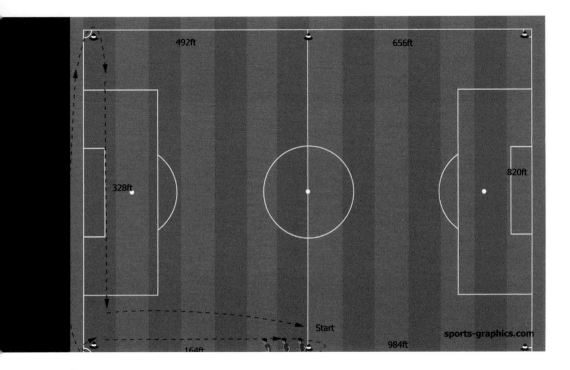

Setup

O   Mark the full field on every corner point with a cone.

Sequence

○ The runs are always started from the starting cone and with 80% sprint (100% full sprint).

○ Sprint back up to the first corner and jog back to the starting cone (50m [164 ft]).

○ Sprint back up to the second corner and jog back to the starting cone (100m [328 ft]).

○ Sprint to the other side of center line and jog back to the start cone (150m [492 ft]).

○ Sprint to the next cone and back to the start cone (200m [656 ft]).

○ Sprint to the next cone and back to the start cone (250m [820 ft]).

○ Sprint a full field and jog a full field (300m [984 ft]).

○ Three-minute water break

○ Sprint to the last cone and jog back to the start cone (250m [820 ft]).

○ Sprint to the next cone and jog back to the start cone (200m [656 ft]).

○ Sprint to the other side of center line and jog back to the start cone (150m [492 ft]).

○ Sprint back up to the second corner and jog back to the starting cone (100m [328 ft]).

○ Sprint back up to the first corner and jog back to the starting cone (50m [164 ft]).

Soccer: The 6-Week Plan

Main Exercise 1: Pass the Ball Between the Cone Goals (10 minutes)

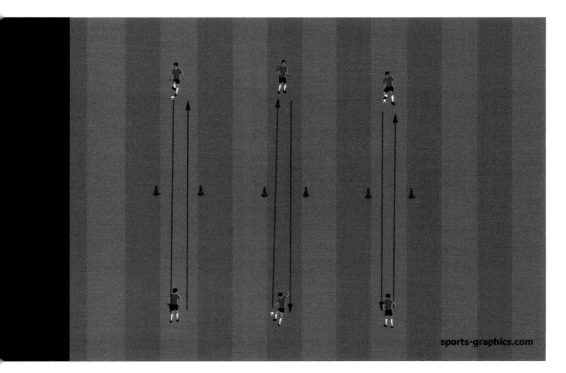

Setup
O   Divide players into pairs.
O   Give each pair one ball and one 5-foot goal marked with cones.

Sequence
O   The players pass the ball to each other through the cone goal.

Tips
O   After the pyramid run, your players need to keep the concentration and focus high and passes precise.

Main Exercise 2: Back Four Example Moves (3 minutes)

Setup
O   Divide players into two groups of eight (four defenders and four offensive players).
O   Position the four defenders across from the four offensive players.
O   The offensive side begins with the ball.

Sequence
O   If player A has the ball, player 1 moves from the defensive line out to attack the offensive players.
O   The other defensive players then move to the left to close the spaces and to support player 1.
O   If player A passes to player B, player 1 must quickly return to the defensive line and player 2 moves out to guard player B.
O   When player 2 moves out, players 1, 3, and 4 must move in to close the spaces and to support player 2.

3

Main Exercise 1: Defensive Line 3-v-3 Individual Tactics (20 minutes)

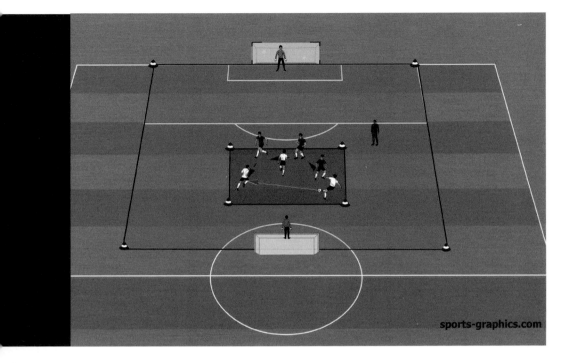

Setup

○   Use cones to mark out two fields (one on each half), as wide as the 18-yard box and 131 feet long. Place a goal at each end of these fields.

○   In the center of each field, mark out a 32-by-32-foot box.

○   Divide players into teams of three.

Sequence

O   Two teams play in the middle field. If the ball goes into the side, start a new attack with a new ball.

O   The attacking team uses skill to get through the defensive line to score a goal.

O   The defending team defends the posterior line about 72 feet in front of the goal through skill, mutual coaching, and sliding out.

O   The defending team should not run behind the defensive line; they need to win the ball in front of this line.

O   Winning the ball can be countered and sent across the opponent's posterior line, and can even score a goal.

Tips

O   The players should hold approximately 72 feet in front of the goal line, move together, coach each other, double up, and come in possession of the ball.

O   If the player in possession of the ball is in trouble, defensive teammates should immediately move adjacent to the defender to get the ball. Now the offensive player is boxed in and has an open side where the second defender can attack and steal the ball.

O   It is important to always stay close to the opposing players.

O   The coach should pay attention to the tactical details and interject when necessary to help players improve and eventually be able to coach themselves as in a gameplay situation.

Main Exercise 2: 5-v-5 With Focus on the Back Four (20 minutes)

sports-graphics.com

Setup

○ Divide the field into two half fields.

○ Make each field narrower to make it easier for the back four.

○ Place two cone goals in 16 feet in front of the midline.

○ Divide the players into two teams of five.

Sequence

○ The defensive players defend their goal by using clever moves.

○ If the defending team wins the ball, a defensive player can score a goal by dribbling through one of the two cone goals.

○ When there is a loss of possession, the offensive players must quickly switch and defend the two cone goals.

○ If the ball is out, start a new round of attack.

○ The game continues until there have been 20 attacks.

Completion Game: (10 minutes)

Setup

O   Use cones to mark out a field from the 18-yard line to the 18-yard line box.

O   Each end line has one goal.

O   Split players into two teams.

Sequence

O   Play a free game with unlimited touches and offsides.

O   The losing team picks up the cones and cleans up the field.

3

WEEK 3, DAY 10

Warm-Up 1: Short Running Warm-Up (5-7 minutes)

Warm-Up 2: Pyramid Run (30 minutes)

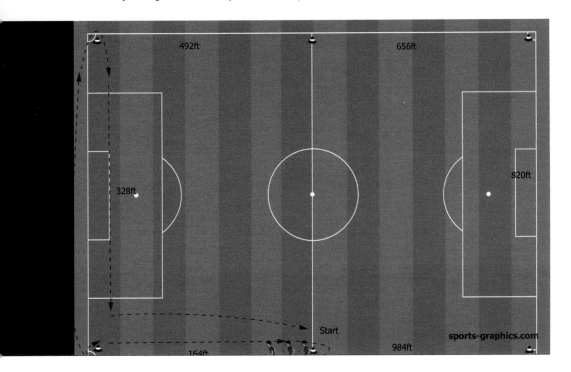

Setup

O   Mark the full field on every corner point with a cone.

Sequence

O The runs are always started from the starting cone and with 80% sprint (100% full sprint).

O Sprint back up to the first corner and jog back to the starting cone (50m [164 ft]).

O Sprint back up to the second corner and jog back to the starting cone (100m [328 ft]).

O Sprint to the other side of center line and jog back to the start cone (150m [492 ft]).

O Sprint to the next cone and back to the start cone (200m [656 ft]).

O Sprint to the next cone and back to the start cone (250m [820 ft]).

O Sprint a full field and jog a full field (300m [984 ft]).

O Three-minute water break

O Sprint to the last cone and jog back to the start cone (250m [820 ft]).

O Sprint to the next cone and jog back to the start cone (200m [656 ft]).

O Sprint to the other side of center line and jog back to the start cone (150m [492 ft]).

O Sprint back up to the second corner and jog back to the starting cone (100m [328 ft]).

O Sprint back up to the first corner and jog back to the starting cone (50m [164 ft]).

3

Main Exercise 1: Pass the Ball Between the Cone Goals (10 minutes)

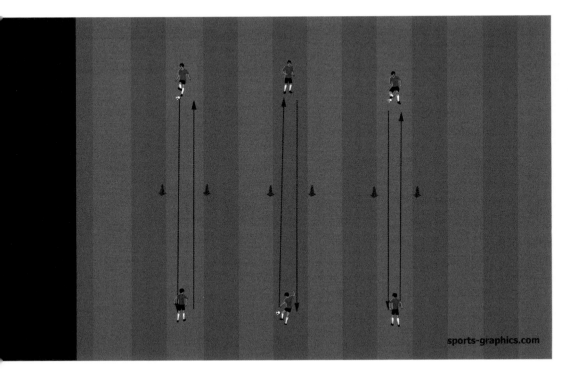

sports-graphics.com

Setup
○ Divide players into pairs.
○ Give each pair one ball and one 5-foot goal marked with cones.

Sequence
○ The players pass the ball to each other through the cone goal.

Tips
○ After the pyramid run, your players need to keep the concentration and focus high and passes precise.

Main Exercise 2: Back Four Example Moves (3 minutes)

Setup

O   Divide players into two groups of eight (four defenders and four offensive players).

O   Position the four defenders across from the four offensive players.

O   The offensive side begins with the ball.

Sequence

O   If player A has the ball, player 1 moves from the defensive line out to attack the offensive players.

O   The other defensive players then move to the left to close the spaces and to support player 1.

O   If player A passes to player B, player 1 must quickly return to the defensive line and player 2 moves out to guard player B.

O   When player 2 moves out, players 1, 3, and 4 must move in to close the spaces and to support player 2.

3

Main Exercise 2: 5-v-5 With Focus on the Back Four (20 minutes)

sports-graphics.com

Setup
- O   Divide the field into two half fields.
- O   Make each field narrower to make it easier for the back four.
- O   Place two cone goals in 16 feet in front of the midline.
- O   Divide the players into two teams of five.

Sequence
- O   The defensive players defend their goal by using clever moves.
- O   If the defending team wins the ball, a defensive player can score a goal by dribbling through one of the two cone goals.
- O   When there is a loss of possession, the offensive players must quickly switch and defend the two cone goals.
- O   If the ball is out, start a new round of attack.
- O   The game continues until there have been 20 attacks.

Conclusion: (10 minutes)

sports-graphics.com

Setup

○ Use cones to mark out a field from the 18-yard line to the 18-yard line box.

○ Each end line has one goal.

○ Split players into two teams.

Sequence

○ Play a free game with unlimited touches and offsides.

○ The losing team picks up the cones and cleans up the field.

3

 ## WEEK 4, DAY 11

Warm-Up 1: Acting Quickly and Warming Up (7 minutes)

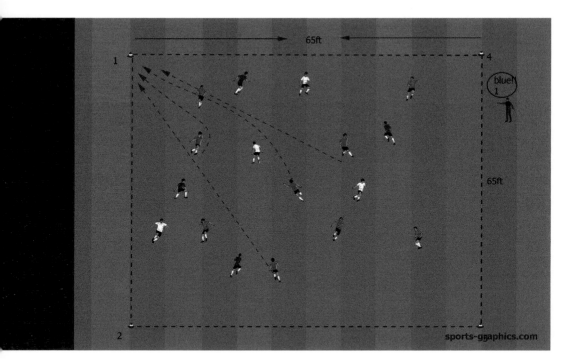

Setup

O   Mark out a 65-by-65-foot field.

O   Divide players into four groups.

O   Each player in a group gets the same color cone.

Sequence

O   The players all run in the field holding their cones.

O   On a command from the coach, teams must run to a corner of the square.

O   Each team must be in a corner; there cannot be two teams in a corner.

O   Players must be in place as quickly as possible; they must find the other members in their group and then decide on a corner together.

O   Players may not arrange before the coach's signal.

O   The team that gets into a corner last must do 10 push-ups.

Warm-Up 2: Hunter (7 minutes)

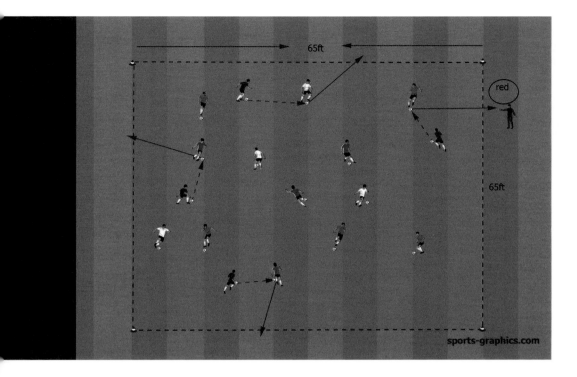

Setup

O   Mark out an 81-by-81-foot field.

O   Divide players into four groups of four.

O   Give each player a ball.

Sequence

O   The teams dribble randomly in the field, using different dribbling tasks.

O   On a command from the coach (e.g., "Blue!"), the designated team tries to knock away the other players' balls.

O   Once the team has successfully knocked away all the other players' balls, a new round begins.

Main Exercise 1: Midfield Pressing From the Compactness (20 minutes)

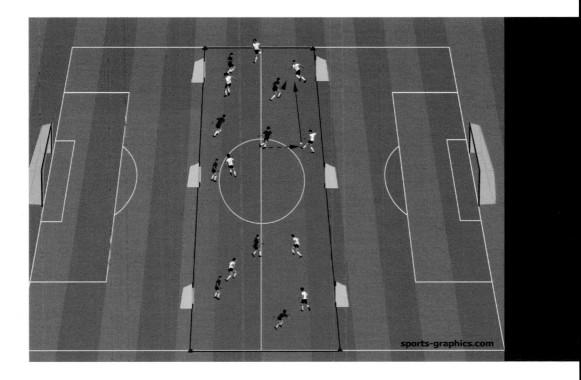

Setup

○   Mark out a field that is about 50 feet behind the center line and the end lines of the playing field.

○   Place three mini goals on both sides of the end lines or use cones to mark the mini goals.

○   Divide the players into two teams.

Sequence

○   Play with tactical guidelines from the compactness of the field (i.e., pressing).

○   Goals can only be made in the opponent's half.

○   Which team scored more goals?

4

Main Exercise 2: Midfield Pressing (15 minutes)

Setup
○   Divide the players into two teams and place players in their positions.

Sequence
○   Game structures for midfield pressing are simulated and rehearsed.

○   All players must stay with the ball as fast as possible and stand compactly.

○   Player 8 and player 10 should not stand too deep, but deep enough so the ball cannot be played through the half field.

○   Run to player 11 so that the defender has to play outwards.

○   Player 8 and player 10 should stand so that the opponent can play to the fullbacks, and when the ball is played there, run aggressively to pressure the opponent.

○   When the outer centerfield player starts running, the other player must move in and push so that no gaps will occur.

Main Exercise 3: Double (15 minutes)

Setup

O   Divide players into two teams and place players in their positions.

Sequence

O   Player 5 runs to the opponent player (not too fast), waits, slows down the speed of
    the opposing player, and places him outwards.

O   Player 8 comes in to help, doubles up, and runs to the open side.

O   There is no chance for the opponent to get out of there—their own team wins
    the ball!

4

Soccer: The 6-Week Plan

Main Exercise 4: Compact Defending (20 minutes)

Setup

O   Mark out a 230-by-130-foot playing field.

O   Place a goal on the baseline, and make two or three cone goals about 23 feet wide
    on the opposite end of the field.

O   Make a 16-foot wide cone goal on the attacker position.

O   Make a cone goal on each side on the half outward positions.

O   Make a cone goal close behind the center line.

O   Divide the players into two teams.

Sequence

O   The offensive team plays out from the rear and tries to dribble through one of the
    two cone goals at the opposite end of the field, which counts as two goals.

O   If the offensive team dribbles through one of the other cone goals, it counts as one goal.

O   The defensive team tries to defend the cone goals, get the ball, switch forward
    quickly, and shoot a goal.

O   When the defensive team loses the ball, quickly switch back and take positions.

- Player 11 is responsible for defending the front goal.
- Players 7 and 8 defend the outer cone goals and run to the outer opponent player.
- Player 9 defends the cone goal in the middle and provides the pass paths in the middle.
- Players 6 and 10 defend both goals in the rear.

Conclusion: End Game (10 minutes)

sports-graphics.com

Setup

- Mark a playing field from one penalty area to the other.
- Place a large goal on both end lines.
- Divide the players into two teams.

4

Sequence

- Play a free game with offside.
- The losing team has to clean up the field.

WEEK 4, DAY 12

Warm-Up: Run-In, Coordination, and Passing Game (10 minutes)

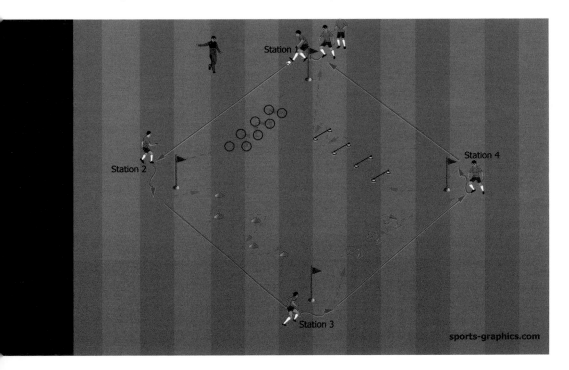

Setup

○   Use four cones to mark a 32-by-32-foot square.

○   Set up stations between the cones:

○   Station 1: Six rings

○   Station 2: Five cones in a zigzag formation

○   Station 3: Three hurdles

○   Station 4: Five bars in a row 2 feet apart

○   Each cone has two or three players. If the number of players requires, set up another box.

○   Start with a ball at the first station.

Sequence

○ Player 1 passes to player 2 and then runs over the rings course, stepping in each ring.

○ Player 2 touches the ball with a contact to the side, passes to player 3, and then runs around the hurdles course with quick side steps.

○ Player 3 touches the ball with a contact to the side, passes to player 4, and then jumps over the hurdles.

○ Player 4 touches the ball with a contact to the side, passes to the next player, and then runs through the bars on the ground.

4

Main Exercise 1: Baseball (20 minutes)

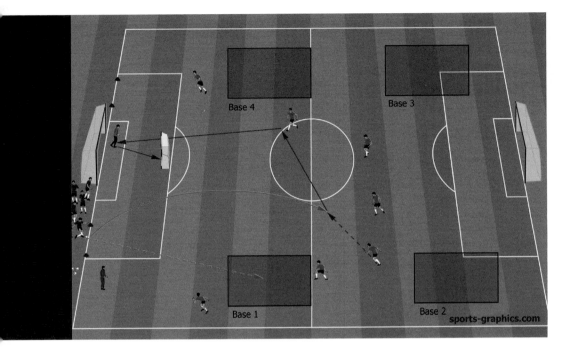

Setup

- ○ Use cones to mark off four bases.
- ○ Divide players into two teams of eight.
- ○ Team A begins on the first tee point and team B is distributed in the field.
- ○ Set up a mini goal in the penalty spot.

Sequence

- ○ The first player on team A shoots a stationary ball into the field and runs to the first base.
- ○ Team B tries to stop the ball and kick it into the mini goal.
- ○ The first player not on the first base is out and goes to the end of the line.
- ○ As soon as team B has formed again, the second player from team A shoots.
- ○ There should never be two players on the same base!
- ○ A home run is worth 10 points; a normal target run is worth one point.
- ○ Play two 8-minute games.

Main Exercise 2: 4-v-4-v-4 Play Form (40 minutes)

sports-graphics.com

Setup

O Mark out a 54-by-54-foot field.

O Keep players in their teams used in the Baseball exercise.

O Four players from each team are on the field while four players are on the outside line around the field.

Sequence

O Play a free game with unlimited touch.

O The attacking players can have only one touch.

O Play ten 2-minute games.

4

Conclusion: 8-v-8 Game (15 minutes)

Setup

○ Mark out a field between the 18-yard boxes with a goal on both sides.

○ The same eight-player teams play together.

Sequence

○ Play a free game with unlimited touch and offsides.

○ Players should focus on using previously learned tactical defense and midfield behavior in the game.

○ Play with a compact field to practice pressing.

WEEK 4, DAY 13

Warm-Up 1: Passing Game With Obstacles (10 minutes)

4

Setup
- Mark out a 100-by-100-foot field.
- Spread cones throughout the field.
- Have the players find a partner.
- Every pair gets a ball.

Sequence
- The players move around the field and pass balls to each other while avoiding their teammates and the cones.
- Create variations (e.g., double pass with speed change, direction change, only use weaker foot, and so on).

Warm-Up 2: Dribble and Feints (10 minutes)

Setup

O   Mark out a 100-by-100-foot field.

O   Spread cones throughout the field.

O   Every player gets a ball.

Sequence

O   The players dribble their balls around the field and do a feint when they reach a cone.

O   The players must watch for teammates to prevent a clash.

O   Create variations (e.g., different rules on feints, direction change in front of a cone, speed change after a feint, and so on).

Main Exercise 1: Targeted Midfield Pressing in Three Steps (25 minutes)

Step 1: Pinch Off

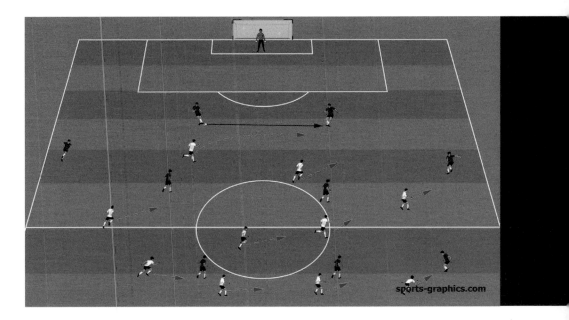

Sequence

O   The offensive goalie begins the game with a throw-in or a pass to the right central
    defender (player 4).

O   The right central defender plays the ball to the left central defender (player 5).

O   As soon as the left central defender gets into the midfield pressing zone, the central
    spire (player 9) of the pressing team pinches off the second central defender in a
    curve run, changing the back pass path.

O   Players 6, 8, and 10 of the pressing team change the pass paths in the depth.

O   The outward player (player 7) of the pressing team moves slightly into the middle
    and releases player 3 of the offensive team.

O   The pressing outward player (player 7) delivers the pass path to the outer player
    (player 11) of the offensive team and at the same time provokes a pass to the
    fullback (player 3) which closes the space of the offensive team.

4

Step 2: Inward Steering

Sequence

O   Let the midfield pressing step (player 1) play through until the ball is played to the fullback (player 3) of the offensive team.

O   The pressing outward player (player 7) pushes outward parallel to the pressing line and changes the passing path along the sideline and steers the game setup of the offensive team back inside.

O   Player 9 of the pressing team changes the back pass opportunities to the center defender (player 5) of the offensive team.

O   Player 6 of the pressing team covers sideways and not too close to the pressing victim (the player from whom the ball is taken) of the offensive team.

O   The left outward player (player 11) of the pressing team pushes forward.

O   The four-man defense pressing them moves with the ball, secure against volleys in the depth.

O   The right defender (player 2) of the pressing team stays in the area because the left outward player (player 11) of the offensive team is in the cover shadow of the pressing outward player (player 7) and not available for play.

Step 3: Double to the Back

Sequence

O Let the midfield pressing player play through until the ball is played to the pressing victim (player 8) of the offensive team.

O Player 6 of the pressing team pushes to the pressing victim of the offensive team and prevents an offensive takeover of the ball.

O If the situation allows, player 6 can also directly conquer the ball.

O Player 10 of the pressing team comes to double up on the pressing victim with player 6.

O Player 11 of the pressing team speculates on a pass to player 4 of the offensive team and delivers this path.

O If the fullback (player 3) of the offensive team dribbles the ball into the center or lays down the ball for a volley, then the pressing player (player 7) must force player 3 into a duel or block the volley.

4

Main Exercise 2: 11-v-11 Game on the Entire Field (20 minutes)

Sequence

O Play an 11-v-11 free game with offside and tactical guidelines.

O The focus of the training game is the moving and advancement of the four-man defense. Stay compact (the defense and attack lines stand 98-by-114 feet apart maximum) and target a midfield pressing setup to take possession of the ball.

WEEK 5

 WEEK 5, DAY 14

Warm-Up 1: Short Run and Dribbling (10 minutes)

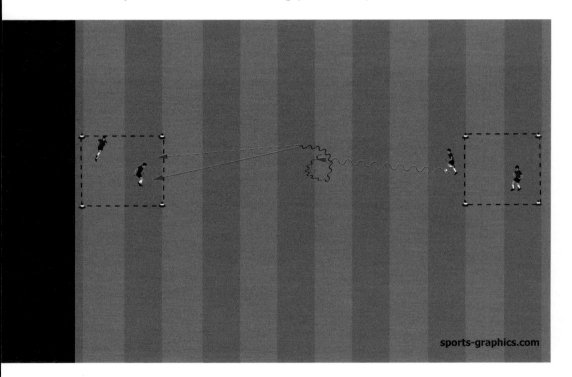

sports-graphics.com

Setup

○ Mark out several 19-by-19-foot fields.

○ Place a cone in between the fields.

○ Assign two players to each field and give them a ball.

Sequence

○ The first player dribbles around the cone at full speed.

○ The player then passes to one of the players at the opposite field.

○ After the pass, he sprints to the other side field.

Soccer: The 6-Week Plan

Warm-Up 2: Volley Ball (7 minutes)

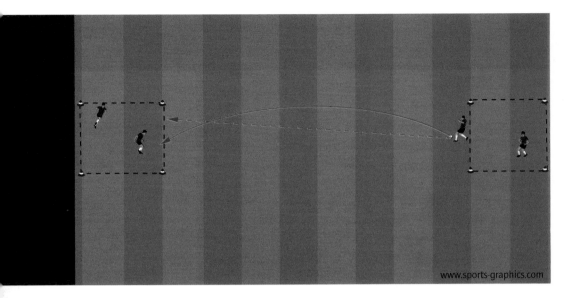

www.sports-graphics.com

Setup

○   Mark out several 19-by-19-foot fields.

○   Place a cone in between the fields.

○   Assign two players to each field and give them a ball.

Sequence

○   The players pass the ball in the box together two or three times.

○   Then a player touches the ball in front and plays a long fly ball to a player on the opposite field.

○   After the long fly ball, the player sprints to the opposite box.

Main Exercise 1: 3-v-2 Majority Situation (10 minutes)

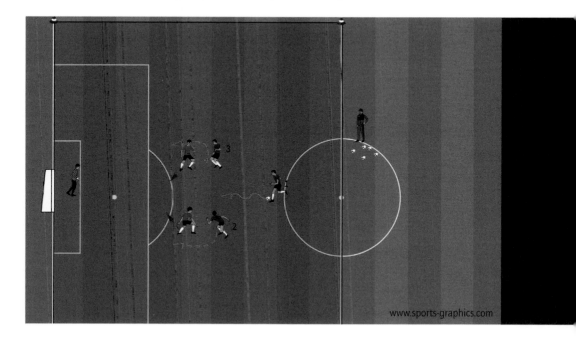

www.sports-graphics.com

Setup

O   This exercise only uses half of the field.

O   Divide the players into offensive and defensive teams.

Sequence

O   Attackers 2 and 3 run to the outside to open the center.

O   Player 1 dribbles the ball to the defender.

O   If the middle is wide open, player 1 can even run to the goal.

O   If the defender is moving to the center, player 1 must dribble toward the defensive player and pass the ball to one of the two attackers in the open space.

5

Main Exercise 2: 1-v-2 and 3-v-2 Game (10 minutes)

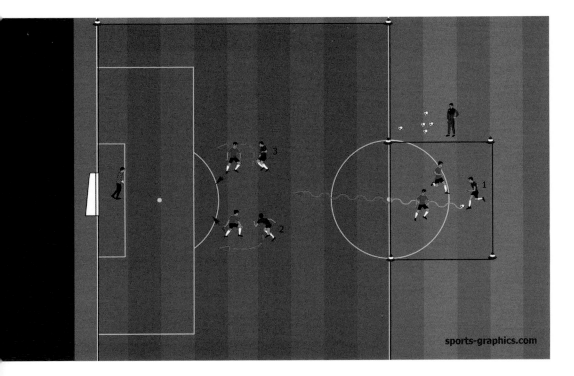

sports-graphics.com

Setup

○   On the midline, mark out a 29-by-29-foot box.

○   Position two defensive players and one offensive player in this box.

○   Position two defensive players and 2 offensive players in front of the 18-yard box.

Sequence

○   In the small field, the offensive player dribbles up to the two defensive players and tries to dribble over the line.

○   The two players that win the ball quickly play a counterattack; only one player may turn.

○   This creates a 3-v-2 situation.

Main Exercise 3: 1-v-1 and Crossing Right and Left (15 minutes)

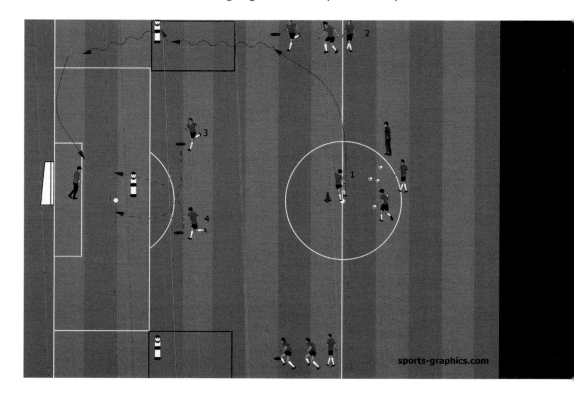

Setup
- O   Mark a 32-by-32-foot field on both sides of the field.
- O   Place one defender in each field and one defender in the penalty box.

Sequence
- O   Player 1 passes a high ball to player 2.
- O   Player 2 controls the ball and plays 1-v-1 against the defenders in the box.
- O   Player 2 then runs with the ball to the base line and passes the ball to the strikers.
- O   Players 3 and 4 (attackers) use the pass and then run.
- O   The defender attempts to prevent the player in the penalty area from scoring by using good position.
- O   If the strikers don't score enough goals, play without the defender to create more success stories.

5

Main Exercise 4: Offensive Attack From Outside (15 minutes)

Setup
O   This exercise is played on half of the field.

O   Position the players as shown in the figure.

Sequence
O   Player 1 passes to player 3 and moves into the penalty box.

O   Player 3 dribbles the ball to the outside defenders.

O   At the same time, player 2 runs behind player 3 in a full sprint.

O   Player 3 adjusts outward to player 2.

O   Player 2 passes the ball in the penalty box.

O   During the flank, two attackers cross to score a goal.

Conclusion: Goals After Cross Balls (15 minutes)

Setup

○ This exercise is played on half of the field with a goal at either end.

○ Divide players into two teams.

○ In each corner, mark a 22-by-16-foot area.

Sequence

○ Play a free game with no defender in the cross ball box and no challenges in the box and in the penalty box.

○ Goals scored after cross balls count twice.

○ Normal goals count as one goal.

5

Soccer: The 6-Week Plan

 WEEK 5, DAY 15

Warm-Up: Run In With Different Exercises (10 minutes)

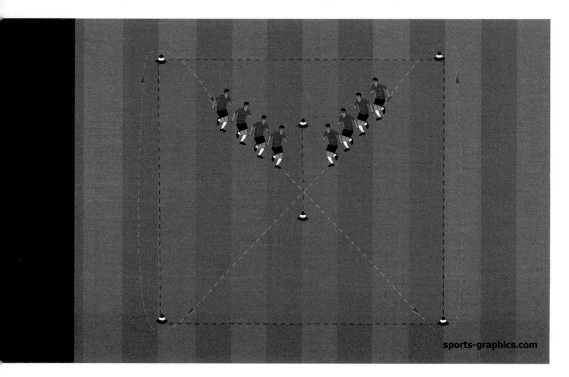

sports-graphics.com

Setup

○ Mark out a 48-by-48-foot field with a 9-foot cone goal.

○ Divide players into two groups; one group starts from the left cone while the other group starts from the right cone.

Sequence

○ On a coach's signal, both groups run at a moderate pace toward opposing cones.

○ From there, they run diagonally across the field and cross in the middle of the field in zipper-style walking distances.

○ Have players repeat this exercise, adding different exercises, such as stroke coordination, sole speed dribble, and so on.

Main Exercise 1: Speed, Coordination, and Shooting (20 minutes)

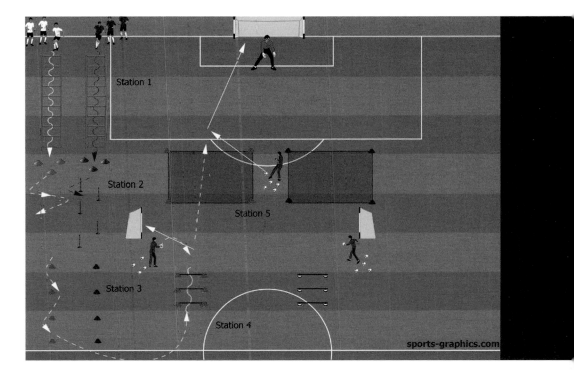

Setup
O   Build an obstacle course with ladders, poles, and mini goals (see figure).

Sequence
O   **Station 1:** Steps or passes (in different rhythms) on the coach's signal.
O   **Station 2:** Tempo dribbling through the slalom poles.
O   **Station 3:** Juggling through the cones.
O   **Station 4:** Pass to the trainer, then skip over the hurdles; the coach throws the ball at head height for players to head back; coach throws the ball at chest height, players bring it under chest control and kick the ball into the mini goal.
O   **Station 5:** Walking through the square. The coach adapts the ball for either player 1 or player 2. The player shoots the ball as quickly as possible to the goal (at least after the second ball contact). The other players attack the player with the ball.

5

Main Exercise 2: Three Different Attacking Moves (30 minutes)

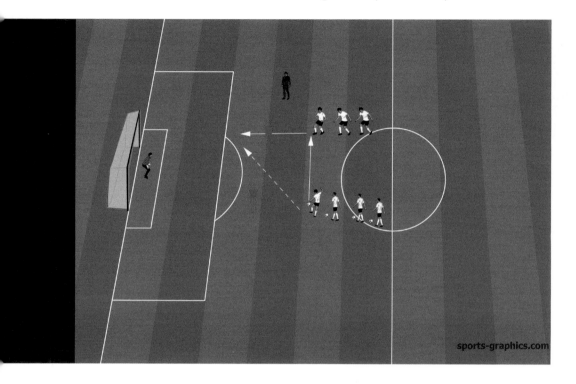

Setup

○   This is exercise is played on half of the field.

○   Position two dolls or rods as defenders about 82 feet in front of the goal.

Sequence

○   Player 1 and player 2 run deep into the defensive side.

○   Player 2 takes the ball and then touches it to the right of the dolls.

○   Player 1 takes the ball and shoots on goal.

○   Make sure that player 1 is in an onside position while receiving the pass from player 2.

Main Exercise 3: Passing Into the Depths After a Double Pass

Setup
- This exercise is played on half of the field.
- Position two dolls or rods as defenders approximately 81 feet in front of the goal.

Sequence
- Player 2 comes to player 1 then, at the same time, passes the ball to player 1.
- Player 2 lets the ball bounce while player 3 runs diagonally into the depth.
- Player 1 passes the ball into the depth, where player 3 has run in.
- Player 2 turns away after letting the ball bounce to player 1, creating free space for player 3, and then runs up in front.
- Player 3 should come toward the goal or pass to player 2.

5

Main Exercise 4: Pass to the Third in the Depth

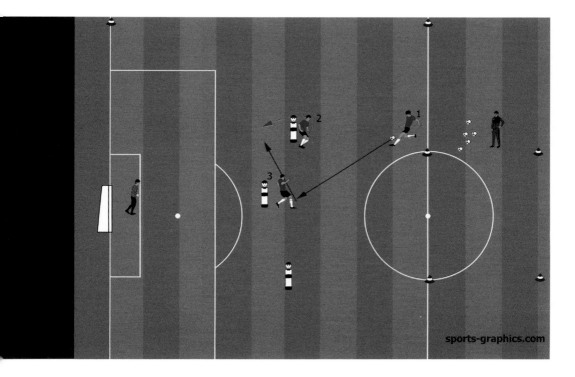

Setup
- ○ This exercise is played on half of the field.
- ○ Position three dolls or rods as defenders in front of the penalty area.

Sequence
- ○ Player 1 passes to player 2, who quickly approaches and acts as if he is going to take the ball but lets the ball run to player 3.
- ○ Player 2 cancels after the pass and runs into the depth.
- ○ Meanwhile, player 3 passes the ball directly to player 2 in the free space.
- ○ Player 2 shoots toward the goal.

Main Exercise 5: Attack Game With Time Limit (20 minutes)

Setup

O   Place three cones near the center line in different positions (see figure).

O   Place two more cones about 16 feet behind the center line in the outward positions (see figure).

O   Divide players into an offensive team and a defensive team.

Sequence

O   Three players on the attacking team spread to the cones on the center line while two go on the attack.

O   Defending players stand in front of the penalty area and two players spread to the two cones behind the center line.

O   The goalie plays a long ball to one of the three players on the cones.

O   The player takes the ball from the air and then the attacking team has 10 seconds to get to the goal to score.

O   When one of the attacking player takes the ball after the long ball from the goalie, the other two players are allowed to sprint in to help the defending team.

5

Conclusion: End Game (10 minutes)

Setup

O   Mark out the playing field from penalty area to penalty area.

O   Place a large goal on each of the two end lines.

O   Divide players into two teams (depending on the amount of players).

Sequence

O   Play a free game with offsides.

O   The losing team has to clean up the field.

WEEK 5, DAY 16

Warm-Up 1: Run With Coordination (10 minutes)

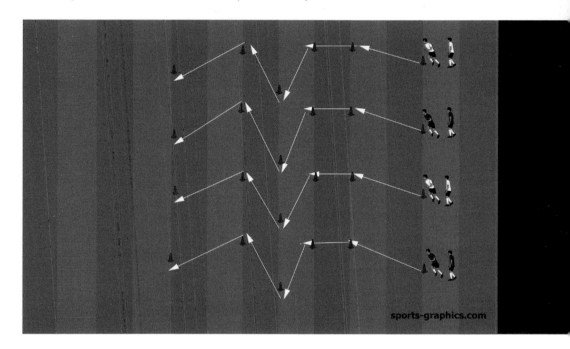

Setup
O   Divide players into four groups.
O   Mark a cone course for every group (see figure).

Sequence
O   From the starting cone to the first cone, players do side-steps.
O   Players do butt kicks from the first cone to the second cone.
O   Players then side step around cones 2, 3, and 4.
O   Players run with high knees from the fourth cone to the end cone.
O   Then they jog back to the starting cone and continue with different exercises (e.g., forwards and backwards running, ankle work, and so on).

5

Warm-Up 2: Pass Game (10 minutes)

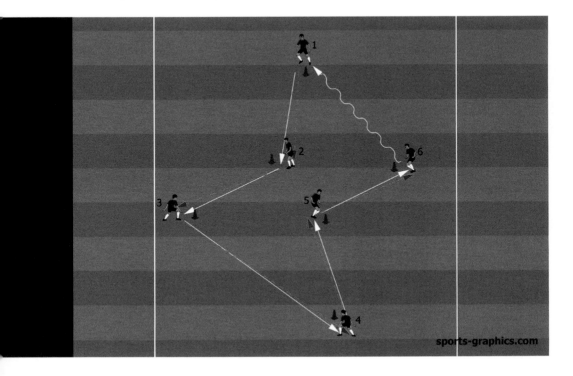

Setup
○ Mark out a field by placing six cones about 32 feet away from each other as seen in the figure; you may need to build more fields, depending on the number of players.
○ One player begins on each cone.

Sequence
○ Player 1 passes to player 2, calls out "Turn around!" and runs after him.
○ Player 2 takes the ball with a contact to the other side, passes to player 3, calls out "Turn around!" and runs after him.
○ Player 3 takes the ball with him to the side, passes to player 4, and runs after him.
○ Player 4 passes the ball directly to player 5, calls out "Turn around!" and runs after him.
○ Player 5 takes the ball with a contact to the side, passes to player 6, and calls out "Turn around!"
○ Player 6 takes the ball with a contact to the side and dribbles the ball to the starting cone.

Main Exercise 1: Goal Shot With Jumps (8 minutes)

Setup

○ Place two goals on the base line and mark the 16-yard line with cones.

○ Place three obstacles on the 16-yard line in front of each goal.

○ Mark the sprinting path with cones (see figure).

○ Make sure the passers have enough balls.

○ Divide the players into two groups.

Sequence

○ On the coach's signal, the first player of each group runs and jumps over the obstacles.

○ After the last obstacle, the player sprints back to the starting cone.

○ When the player is at the cone, he gets a pass from the passer played into the depth.

○ The player sprints into the depth and shoots at the goal.

○ Which group has scored more goals once the time is up?

5

Main Exercise 2: Speed With Goal Shots (8 minutes)

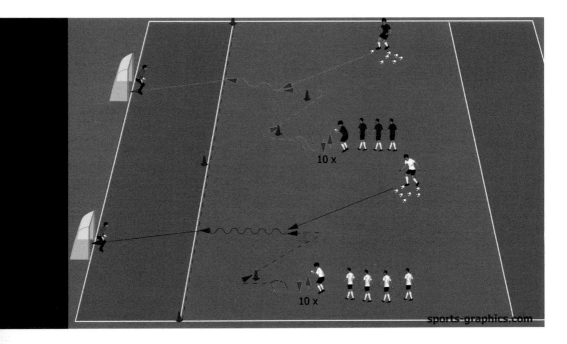

Setup

O   Place two goals on the base line and mark the 16-yard line with cones.

O   Place three obstacles on the 16-yard line in front of each goal.

O   Mark the sprinting path with cones (see figure).

O   Make sure the passers have enough balls.

O   Players should remain in the same two groups used in the previous exercise.

O   Each group should have one medicine ball.

Sequence

O   Holding the medicine ball by their necks, the first players from each team do 10 squats and then throw away the medicine ball.

O   They then jump over the obstacles and sprint to the cone.

O   After the last cone, every player gets a pass from the passer played into the depth.

O   The player sprints into the depth and shoots at the goal.

O   Which group has scored more goals once the time is up?

Main Exercise 3: Goal Shot After Return Run (8 minutes)

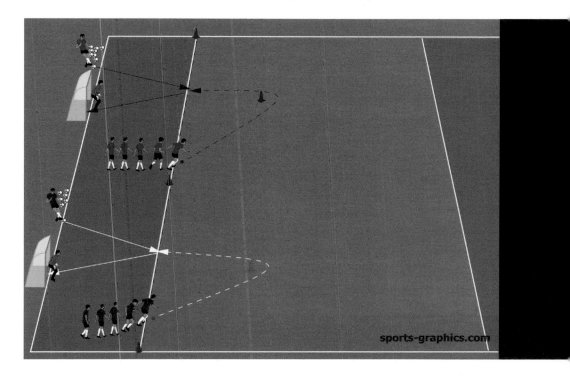

Setup

○ Place two goals on the base line and mark the 16-yard line with cones.

○ Mark the sprinting path in front of the 16-yard line with cones (see figure).

○ Make sure the passers have enough balls next to the goals.

○ Players should remain in the same two groups used in the previous exercise.

Sequence

○ The first player sprints back to the cone and then get a pass from the passer next to the goal.

○ The player then shoots towards the goal.

○ Which group has scored more goals once the time is up?

5

Main Exercise 4: Score Goals on Both Sides (20 minutes)

sports-graphics.com

Setup

O   Mark out a playing field about 40 meters long and 16 meters wide.

O   Place a goal on each base line of the playing field.

O   Divide the players into two teams.

O   The coach has all the balls at the touchline.

Sequence

○ One team defends both goals, while the other team can score at both goals.

○ When winning the ball, the defending team must try to hold the ball as long as possible in their own row.

○ If the ball is shot into touch three times by the defending team, the attacking team gets a penalty kick at the end of the game.

○ If the ball is shot into touch by the attacking team, a new ball is played into the game for the defending team from the outside and the attacking team then gets the ball.

○ Have teams switch objectives after 8 minutes.

○ Which team scores more goals during the exercise?

5

Conclusion: Corner Ball (10 minutes)

Variant 1

Sequence

O   Player 11 and player 9 stand about 7 feet in front of the goal post on the goal line.

O   Players 4 and 5 lurk in the rear area, waiting for a rebound.

O   When player 10 plays in the ball, players 9 and 11 come to about 2 meters in front of the goal and lurk for the ball.

O   Player 6 runs at the height of the shortest post.

O   Player 7 runs to the middle of the goal.

O   Player 8 goes long to the second post.

Tips

O   Players 9 and 11 should only leave the goal line when the ball is played into it. Why? Because at the moment the ball is played in, all opposing players often look at the ball, giving players 9 and 11 1 or 2 seconds to release from the opponent player and reposition, perhaps for a rebound when the ball is extended on the short post.

O   Players 6, 7, and 8 should already cause unrest before the ball is in the area by moving around at all times.

Variant 2 (20 minutes)

Setup

O   Half Field

O   8 offends corner positions

Sequence

O   When player 10 runs to the ball, player 9 runs to the short pole from the goal.

O   Player 10 quickly plays the ball to player 9, which extends the ball.

O   Player 8 runs to the short pole.

O   Player 7 runs more centrally.

O   Player 6 runs to the rear third of the goal.

O   Player 11 walks back.

O   Players 4 and 5 lurk for the rebound.

Tips

- O Player 9 should be a strong head ball player who also has the chance to extend the ball.
- O Players 6, 7, 8, and 11 should cause unrest by randomly running around.
- O The players should speculate on the ball and blindly run through.
- O Watch for the timing of the run-in.

5

Variant 3 (10 minutes)

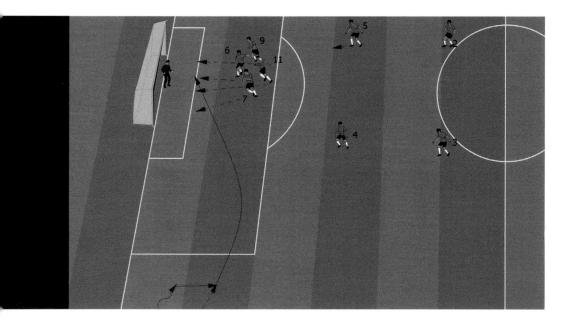

Sequence

○ Player 10 runs around player 8.

○ Player 8 passes to player 10, who sharply flanks the ball in the direction of the goal.

○ Player 7 runs in the direction of the short pole.

○ Player 6 runs more centrally to the goal.

○ Player 11 runs to the rear third of the goal.

○ Player 9 runs to the long pole.

Tips

○   Before player 8 is played to, he waits for the view towards the penalty area, so he has a good overview.

○   Players 6, 7, 9, and 11 cause unrest before the corner ball by randomly running around.

○   The player should run in with a running feint to release himself from the opposing player.

○   Watch for the timing of the run-in.

5

WEEK 6, DAY 17

Warm-Up 1: Strength and Stability Circuit (20 minutes)

O   Each station has two or three players.

O   Players take a 20-30-second break between each station.

O   After one round, players take a 3-minute break.

O   Repeat for a second round.

Exercise 1: Push-Ups

O   Repeat for 20-30 seconds.

Exercise 2: Sit-Ups

O   Repeat for 20-30 seconds.

Exercise 3: Alternating Plank (20 reps)

O   Assume the plank position and alternate slowly lifting the right and left legs.

O   Repeat for 20-30 seconds.

6

Exercise 4: Side Plank

○   Assume a side plank position and then raise and lower the top leg.

○   Repeat for 20-30 seconds.

Exercise 5

○ While lying face down with the feet flexed and toes firmly on the ground, put the hands in the air behind the body and then swing them to the front.

○ Repeat for 20-30 seconds.

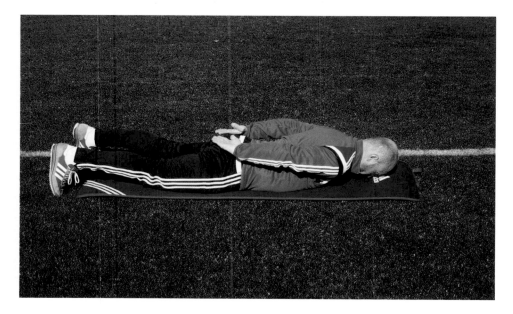

6

Exercise 6

○   Using the forearm and heel for support, lift the body slightly off the ground.

○   While keeping the body in the air, extend the other leg.

○   Repeat for 20-30 seconds.

Exercise 7

○   Start in a forearm plank position.

○   Lift the opposite hand and leg and hold for 20-30 seconds.

○   Repeat with the other hand and leg.

Warm-Up 2: Dribble (5 minutes)

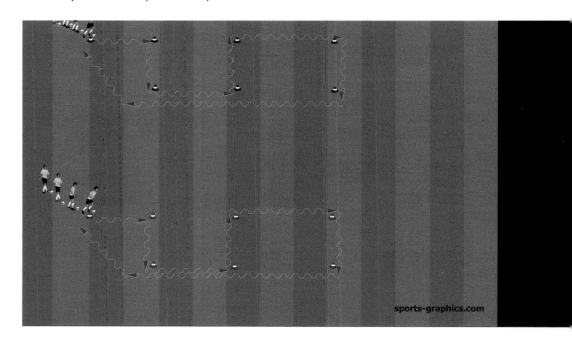

sports-graphics.com

Setup

O   Make two cone courses (see figure).

O   Divide players into two teams.

O   Give each team a ball.

Sequence

O   One player from each team dribbles through the cone course.

O   After the last cone, the ball is given to a teammate

O   Which team reaches finishes the course first?

6

Warm-Up 3: Cap In and Cap Out (5 minutes)

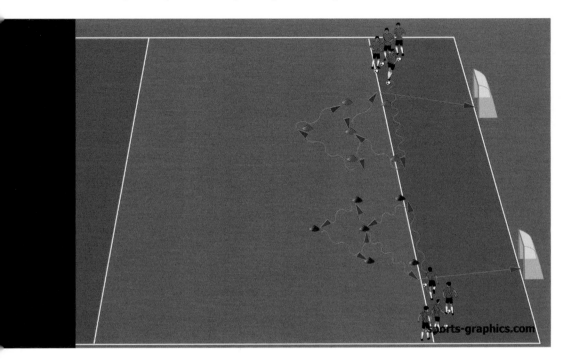

Setup

- O   Make two cone courses (see figure).
- O   Arrange a small goal behind the cone course.
- O   Players remain in their teams from the previous warm-up.

Sequence

- O   One player from every team dribbles through the cone course.
- O   After the last cone, the players attempt to play the ball into the goal.
- O   Which team will score more goals?

Main Exercise: Hold the Ball (25 minutes)

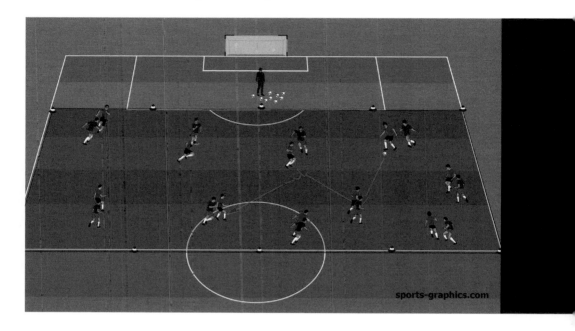

Setup

O   Mark out a field without goals from the penalty area to the halfway line.

O   Divide players into two teams.

Sequence

O   Play a free game in holding the ball.

O   After seven passes without the opponent getting the ball, the team gets a point.

O   Play two 8-minute games.

O   The winner is the team with the most points at the end.

6

Conclusion: 5-v-5 Tournament (40 minutes)

Setup

O   Divide players into teams of five.

O   Mark out a 180-by-81-foot playing field with two large goals.

Sequence

O   Play a tournament of 5-v-5 free games without offsides.

O   Play six 3-minute games with 2 minutes of active recovery between each game.

O   The tournament winner is the team with the most wins.

O   The losing team has to clean up the field.

WEEK 6, DAY 18

Warm-Up 1: Dribble and High Throw (5 minutes)

www.sports-graphics.com

Setup

O   Divide players into groups.

O   Each group has two balls.

Sequence

O   The first players dribble a ball with their feet and throw the other ball in the air so that their eyes look up (players should not lift the head up).

O   The player can let the thrown ball hit the ground once and catch it after.

O   During the action, the other ball is always dribbled by the feet.

6

Warm-Up 2: Dribble and Bounce (10 minutes)

Setup

○   Place three differently colored cones about 3 feet apart. Each group of cones should also have a starting cone.

○   Divide players into two teams.

○   Each team receives two balls.

Sequence

O The coach calls out a color of one of the cones as a start signal.

O The players dribble and bounce the ball at the same time—and as fast as possible—to the corresponding cone, go around it, and then return to the starting cone.

O The player that returns to the starting cone first scores a point for his or her team.

O After playing two or three rounds, which team has the most points?

6

Main Exercise 1: Chain Behaviors (25 minutes)

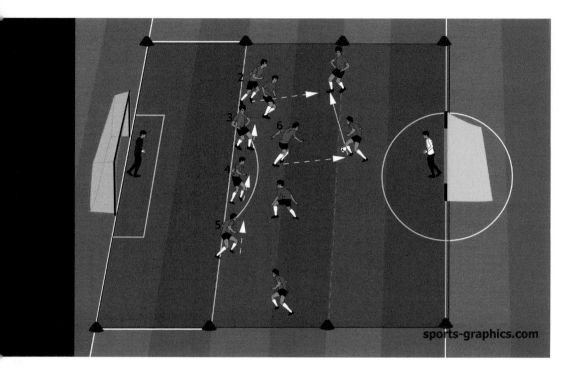

Setup

○   Mark out a 164-by-196-foot playing field.

○   Place two posts approximately 75 feet in front of the goal.

○   Divide players into four teams of five.

Sequence

O Play three 5-minute games of 5-v-5 on 2 goals with tactical specifications.

O The defending team should withdraw to 75 feet in front of the goal when attacked.

O The defending team should hold this position and not run behind the 75-foot line before the ball crosses it. Only when the ball crosses the 75-foot line can the defending team cross it.

O Pay attention to the shifting and the moving of the defending team and correct if necessary.

O Teams switch quickly after winning the ball.

Tip

O Let your midfielders know that the shifting and moving is the same for their positions and that the exercise is also fitting for them.

6

Main Exercise 2: Back Four Gameplay (25 minutes)

Setup

○ Use half of the playing field and make two 22-foot wide cone goals on the center line.

○ Place two posts approximately 75 feet in front of the goal.

○ Divide players into two teams of six.

○ After two rounds, rotate teams with the rest of the players.

Sequence

- ○ Play 6-v-6 using two cone goals with tactical specifications.
- ○ The defending team withdraws to 75 feet in front of the goal with the back four.
- ○ They can only go behind the 75-foot line when the opposing team gets the ball behind the 75-foot line; until that happens they should try to intercept the ball.
- ○ Quickly switch when the ball is won and try to dribble the ball over the opponent goal cones.
- ○ Pay attention to the shifting, fast move out and fast switching.

6

Conclusion: Flank Game (20 minutes)

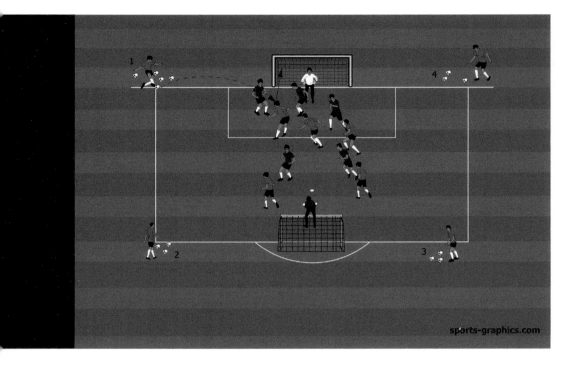

Setup

○   The playing field is the penalty area, baseline, and end of the penalty area with one
    goal each.

○   Position five balls and one player in each of the four corners of the penalty area.

○   Put a goalie in each goal.

Sequence

O   Two teams play against each other in the penalty area with each team defending one goal.

O   The outer players play immediately one after another and always in the same order (see figure) when the ball is offside or a goal is achieved.

O   The corner balls from the penalty area corners go in either flat or high.

O   The teams play each other twice.

O   Which team **scores** the most goals?

Goal of the Exercise

O   Each game goes as long as needed until all five balls from all corners have been played (a total of 20 balls).

O   Everything is included in this exercise: duels, head balls, fast reactions, goal shots, and so on.

6

WEEK 6, DAY 19

**Warm-Up 1: Short Run and Coordination With Three Different Exercises
(15 minutes)**

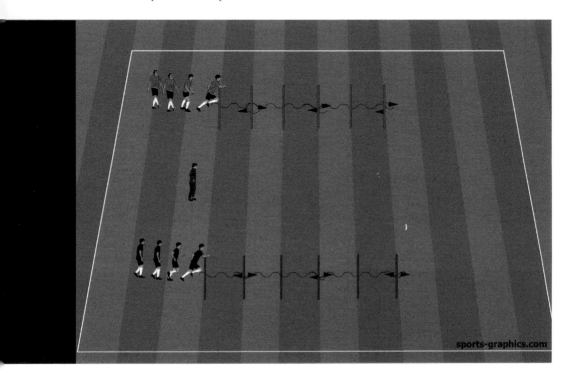

Setup

O   Create two courses of six poles in a row approximately 4 inches apart.

O   Divide players into two groups.

O   Each group stands behind one of the courses.

Sequence

O   Players run over the poles with fast steps and without touching the poles.

O   Players then run back and forth through poles 2,4, and 6.

Warm-Up 2: Coordination Exercise 1

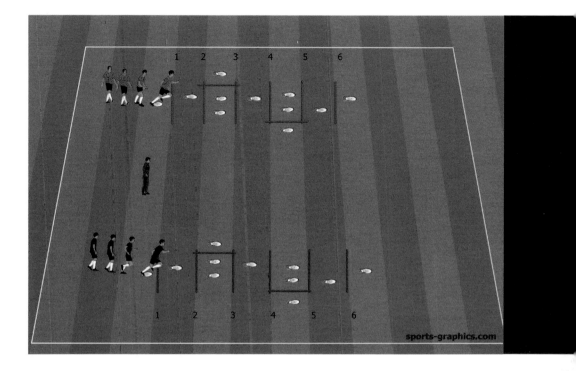

Setup

○   Create two courses of six poles approximately 2.5 feet apart.

○   Place a variant running direction between poles 2 and 3 and between poles 4 and 5.

○   Divide players into two groups.

○   Each group stands behind one of the courses.

6

Sequence

○   Players run over the poles with fast steps and without touching the poles.

○   Players then run back and forth and to the side between poles 2 and 3 and poles 4 and 5.

Warm-Up 3: Coordination Exercise 2

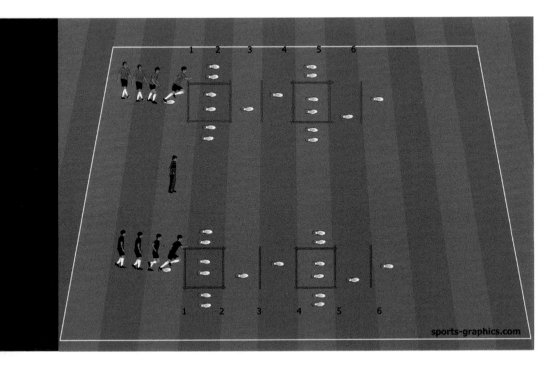

Setup

O   Create two courses of six poles approximately 2.5 feet apart.

O   Place a variant running direction between poles 2 and 3 and between poles 4 and 5.

O   Divide players into two groups.

O   Each group stands behind one of the courses.

Sequence

O   Players run over the poles with fast steps and without touching the poles.

O   Players then run backwards and forwards around the poles between poles 1 and 2 and poles 4 and 5.

Warm-Up 3: Speed of Action After Acclamation (5 minutes)

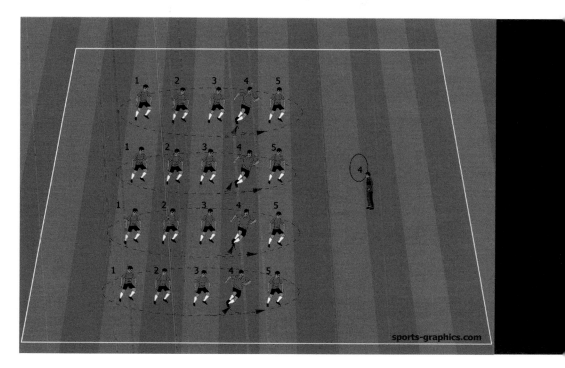

Setup

O   Players count off by fives and then line up in rows corresponding to their numbers
    (e.g., if there are 20 players, there will be four rows of five players).

Sequence

O   The coach calls a number between one and five (e.g., the number 4).

O   The players that have the number 4 have to react fast and sprint around their group
    until they are back to their starting point again.

O   Variations

O   Change paths (e.g., run a slalom through the group and back to the starting point).

O   Perform the exercise with a ball.

6

Main Exercise 1: Corner Play 5-v-2 (10 minutes)

sports-graphics.com

Setup

O   Mark out as many 32-foot fields as needed for the number of players.

O   Position seven players at each field with the two youngest players in the middle.

Sequence

O   The outer players randomly pass the ball to each other.

O   The two players in the middle try to capture the ball.

O   The outer player who loses the ball has to go in the middle.

O   If the ball is touched more than 20 times and the players in the middle did not get the ball, the players in the middle have to do one more round.

Main Exercise 2: Dry Run Midfield Pressing (Take a Run) (5 minutes)

Step 1: Pin Off

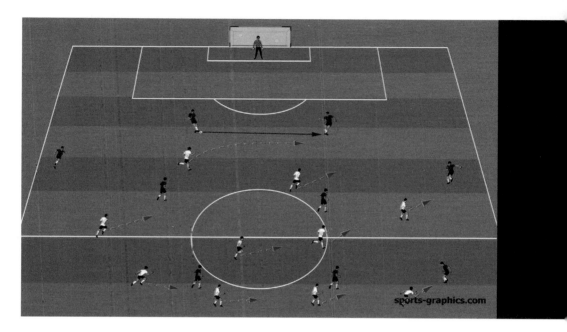

Sequence

- The goalie of the attacking team in control of the ball begins the game with a throw-out or pass to the right central defender (player 4).
- This player plays the ball to the left central defender (player 5).
- As soon as this player reaches the midfield pressing zone, the central striker (player 9) of the pressing team pins off the second central defender in a curvature, changing the back-pass path.
- Teams change the pass paths into depth (see figure).
- The outside player on the pressing team that is closest to the ball (player 7) moves slightly to the middle and consciously releases player 3 of the attacking team.
- The pressing outside player (player 7) delivers a pass path to the other outside player of the attacking team (player 11), and at the same time provokes a pass to the fullback (player 3) that is close to the ball.

6

Step 2: Steer Inward

Sequence

- O Once the ball is played to the fullback of the attacking team (player 3), the pressing outside player (player 7) moves parallel outward to the pressing line and changes the pass path along the sideline, steering the game build-up of the attacking team back to the inside.

- O Player 9 of the pressing team changes the back-pass possibility to the central defender of the attacking team (player 5).

- O Player 6 of the pressing team covers the pressing victim (i.e., the player from whom the ball will be taken) sideways and not too closely.

- O The left outside player (player 11) of the pressing team pushes forward (see figure).

- O The four-man back field defense of the pressing team pushes toward the ball, securing against volleys into depth.

- O The right defender of the pressing team (player 2) stays in the space because the left outside player of the attacking team (player 11) cannot be played to in the cover shade by the pressing outside player (player 7).

Step 3: Doubling to the Back

Sequence

O   Once the ball is played to the pressing victim (player 8), player 6 of the pressing team pushes the pressing victim close and prevents an offensive ball takeaway. If the situation allows, player 6 can also directly capture the ball.

O   Player 10 of the pressing team comes to double the pressing victim with player 6.

O   Player 11 of the pressing team speculates on a pass to player 4 of the attacking team and blocks this way.

O   However, if the fullback dribbles into the center or places the ball in front of him for a volley, then the pressing player 7 must force player 3 into a tackle or block the volley.

6

Main Exercise 3: Five Different Offensive Actions With Shot on the Goal
(25 minutes)

Offensive Action 1

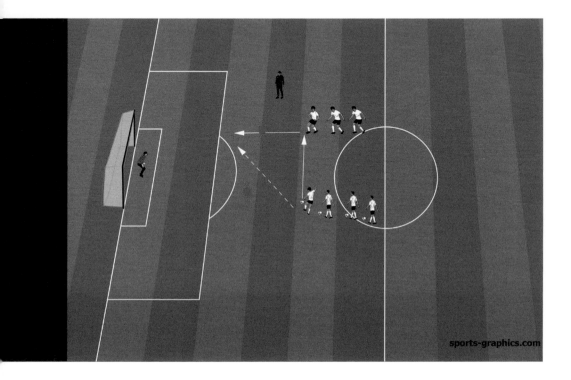

Setup

○   Arrange two dolls or rods as a defensive player about 82 feet in front of the goal.

○   Using a half-court field.

Sequence

○   Player 1 passes to player 2 and runs into the depth behind the defense.

○   Player 2 takes the ball and passes past the dolls on the right into the depth.

○   Player 1 takes the ball and kicks towards the goal.

○   Be aware that player 1 does not stand offsides while receiving the pass from player 2.

Offensive Action 2

sports-graphics.com

Setup
○ Play using a half-court field.
○ Place three dolls or rods as defensive players in front of the penalty area.

Sequence
6

○ Player 1 passes to player 2 who approaches and fakes that he will take the ball, but lets the ball roll to player 3.
○ Player 2 breaks up after faking and runs into the depth.
○ Player 3 passes the ball directly into the free space to player 2.
○ Player 2 kicks towards the goal.

Offensive Action 3

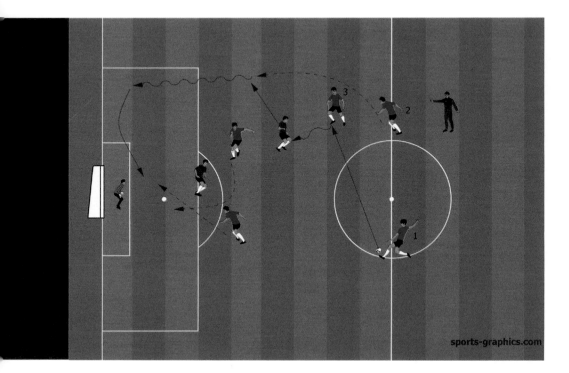

sports-graphics.com

Setup

- O   Play using a half-court field.
- O   Position the players for both sides as seen in the figure.

Sequence

- O   Player 1 passes to player 3 and runs up to the penalty area.
- O   Player 3 dribbles the ball to the fullback.
- O   Player 2 sprints to follow behind player 3.
- O   Player 3 passes then runs outward into the path of player 2.
- O   Player 2 flanks into the penalty area.
- O   During the flank, both attackers cross and try to score a goal.

Offensive Action 4

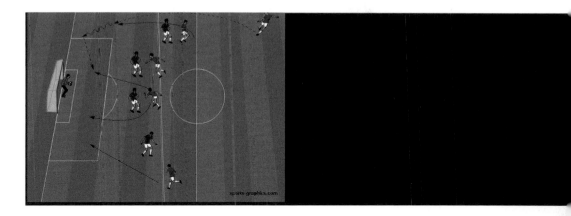

Setup

O   Playing using a half-court field.

O   Assign offensive and defensive players.

Sequence

O   Five offensive players play against four defenders.

O   Player 2 approaches quickly and then runs into the depth.

O   Player 1 plays the ball into the depth once player 2 has made space behind him.

O   Player 2 gets the ball into the path and dribbles to the baseline where he then flanks the ball into the penalty area.

O   Before player 2 flanks the ball into the penalty area, players 3 and 4 cross and run to the penalty area (one to the short post and the other to the second post).

O   Player 5 also comes into the penalty area.

O   If too few goals are shot, make the defensive player only partially active.

6

Offensive Action 5

Setup

O Make a large goal on a playing field from penalty area to penalty area and on both penalty area lines.

O Divide players into two teams.

Sequence

O Play a free game.

O When the ball is hit out on the side, there will be no throw-in, but a free side kick.

O The coach determines from where and how many free side kicks are made.

Conclusion: Reminder of the Three Corner Ball Variants (10 minutes)

Variant 1

Sequence

○ Player 11 and player 9 stand about 7 feet in front of the goal post on the goal line.

○ Players 4 and 5 lurk in the rear area, waiting for a rebound.

○ When player 10 plays in the ball, players 9 and 11 come to about 2 meters in front of the goal and lurk for the ball.

○ Player 6 runs at the height of the shortest post.

○ Player 7 runs to the middle of the goal.

○ Player 8 goes long to the second post.

6

Tips

○ Players 9 and 11 should only leave the goal line when the ball is played into it. Why? Because at the moment the ball is played in, all opposing players often look at the ball, giving players 9 and 11 1 or 2 seconds to release from the opponent player and reposition, perhaps for a rebound when the ball is extended on the short post.

○   Players 6, 7, and 8 should already cause unrest before the ball is in the area by moving around at all times.

Variant 2: (20 minutes)

Sequence

○   When player 10 runs to the ball, player 9 runs to the short pole from the goal.

○   Player 10 quickly plays the ball to player 9, which extends the ball.

○   Player 8 runs to the short pole.

○   Player 7 runs more centrally.

○   Player 6 runs to the rear third of the goal.

○   Player 11 walks back.

○   Players 4 and 5 lurk for the rebound.

Tips

○   Player 9 should be a strong head ball player who also has the chance to extend the ball.

○   Players 6, 7, 8, and 11 should cause unrest by randomly running around.

○   The players should speculate on the ball and blindly run through.

○   Watch for the timing of the run-in.

Variant 3: (10 minutes)

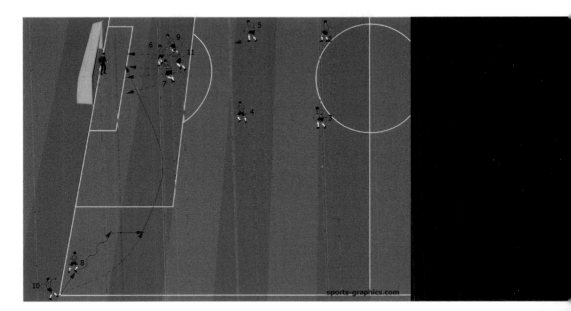

Sequence

- O Player 10 runs around player 8.
- O Player 8 passes to player 10, who sharply flanks the ball in the direction of the goal.
- O Player 7 runs in the direction of the short pole.
- O Player 6 runs more centrally to the goal.
- O Player 11 runs to the rear third of the goal.
- O Player 9 runs to the long pole.

6

Tips

- O Before player 8 is played to, he waits for the view towards the penalty area, so he has a good overview.
- O Players 6, 7, 9, and 11 cause unrest before the corner ball by randomly running around.
- O The player should run in with a running feint to release himself from the opposing player.
- O Watch for the timing of the run-in.

GOAL SHOT TRAINING

SIXTEEN METHODS TO MORE SCORING

With these tips, the goal shot will not be a problem anymore and instead will be a lot of fun for your players! Goal shot training is not only fun for grown-ups, but especially for kids. Why? The scoring of goals is a successful experience for players and that is fun!

What can you do as a trainer to prevent boredom? Here are four important factors on how you can influence this as a coach:

O   Divide players into small groups to avoid long waiting times.

O   Choose age-appropriate distances so the goal success rate will be high. It should be over 50%!

O   Create enthusiasm through competitions during the goal shot training (i.e., keep track of which group scores the most goals)!

O   Vary the goal shot training week by week; you will keep up the players' enthusiasm this way.

At the goal shot training, make sure that your players always learn how to shoot with both feet. This is often a big shortcoming that is hard to learn later on.

How do you explain this exercise to your players in the most effective way?

O   It is important to explain the exercise as quickly as possible because the players do not want to wait, they want to play!

O   Use still images to show your players how to shoot the ball in the best way.

O   Do a test run to see if every player understands the exercise.

As a trainer, make sure that your players correctly perform the goal shot. What should you watch out for?

O   Is the supporting leg close and next to the ball?

O   Does the toe of the supporting foot face the impact direction?

O   Is the player's ankle fixed?

O   Did the player hit the ball in the center?

O   Does the toe of the shooting foot point to the ground?

- Does the leg swing in a straight line to the ball after the goal shot?
- Avoid making too many corrections at once because the player will lose their interest. Just give your players some tips!
- Is the span of the successful experiences suitable? Change it if necessary.
- Are the waiting times too long?
- Can the players perform the exercise? If it is too easy or too hard, change it.

How can you correctly and specifically establish your goal shot training and improve your players step by step? Goal shots happen in every game and need to be trained. There are a few variations to focus on during the goal shot training (e.g., from different positions, as an instep, inward dropkick, outstep, hip shot, overhead kick, and so on).

6

The training must correctly and specifically teach these elements to your players. You have to check for different components during the goal shot training (e.g., the shooting force). The shooting force is a result of the combination of strength and technique; however, it does not mean that the player shoots harder if the player uses a lot of strength for a goal shot. The correct technical movement pattern is much more important and must be the main focus of the training. The accuracy of the goal shot is another important point. Unfortunately, the accuracy often suffers because of the maximum physical effort. The technique variation of goal shots during the goal shot training is also necessary. The goal shot training must be established step by step. The next step, like the goal shot under opponent pressure, should be trained once the players have mastered the goal shot techniques. This training form is close to a real game and should only be trained when the goal shot techniques are mastered.

As a trainer, you should know how to correctly and specifically teach your players these goal shot techniques without overstressing the players, so they are able to dramatically improve themselves. In addition, it is important to know the methodical ways of the goal shot training that help on your players. There are eight ways to do this.

Eight Methodical Ways to Learn and Improve the Goal Shot

- Pre-exercises for the goal shot training
- Goal shot volley from the hand
- Stationary ball
- From dribbling
- Goal shot after receiving and taking
- Goal shot after passing
- Competitive training 1 (e.g., not enough or too much defending behavior)
- Competitive training 2 (e.g., 1-v-1 or complex playing forms with many goal shots)

Exercise 1: Pre-Exercise for the Goal Shot (2 minutes)

Goal of the Exercise
O   Foot posture of the instep (foot position points downward)

Setup
O   Every player gets one ball.

Sequence
O   Players dribble the ball with the instep and play it straight ahead with every step.

6

Further Pre-Exercises
O   Juggle.
O   Pull the ball back with the heel and play it forward with the instep.
O   Play the ball up from the hand.

Exercise 2: Volley from the Hand (3-5 minutes)

Goal of the Exercise

O   Preliminary stage of the volley shot

O   Correct foot posture and where the ball must be hit (in the center)

Setup

O   Divide players into teams of two.

O   Mark out two lines about 13 feet apart.

O   Players stand across from each other.

Sequence

O   The players play the ball to each other from the hand, alternately with the right and left foot at chest height.

O   Which team can perform 15 passes the fastest without the partner having to take a step?

O   This exercise can be extended by shooting the ball with a volley shot from the hand to the goal.

Exercise 3: Stationary Ball (5-7 minutes)

sports-graphics.com

Goal of the Exercise

O   Learning of the instep shot with accuracy

Setup

O   Divide players into teams of two.

O   Each team gets a ball.

O   The players stand about 30-50 feet apart across from each other.

O   Set up a cone goal 3-6 feet wide in the middle of every team.

6

Sequence

O   Players alternately play the ball to each other with the right and left instep through the cone goal.

O   Who is first team to play 15 passes through the cone goal?

O   The distance and size of the cone goals may be varied to make the exercise more difficult or easier as necessary.

Exercise 4: Goal Shot From Dribbling (15 minutes)

Goal of the Exercise
O   Maintain correct shooting technique despite the time pressure
O   Goal shot after dribbling

Setup
O   Place two goals next to each other; each goal has a goalie.
O   Divide players into two groups.
O   Mark a starting cone and a shooting line for each team.

Sequence
O   Two players play against each other. At the coach's signal, the players dribble to the shooting line and take a shot on goal.
O   The team whose player dribbles first to the shooting line after the signal from the coach gets a point.
O   Every goal scored is a point for the respective team.
O   Which group has more points in the end?

Exercise 5: Goal Shot After Receiving and Taking (10 minutes)

sports-graphics.com

Goal of the Exercise
○   Take the ball and shoot with the second contact
○   Shooting technique after receiving and taking the ball

Setup
○   Place a cone offset to the right next to the goal where the players are positioned   6
    with the ball.
○   Place a cone about 30 feet in front of the goal where one player stands.

Sequence
○   Player A passes the ball to player B.
○   Player B takes the ball into the direction of the goal and shoots at the goal.
○   Which player shoots the most goals?

Exercise 6: Shoot Directly After the Pass (10 minutes)

sports-graphics.com

Goal of the Exercise
O   Direct shot after the pass
O   Timing to the ball for the direct goal shot

Setup
O   Place a cone next to the goal with a player and ball.
O   Place a cone as a starting point for the shooter about 40 feet in front of the goal.

Sequence
O   Player A passes the ball to player B.
O   Player B runs from the starting cone towards the ball and shoots at the goal.
O   Which player scores the most goals?

Exercise 7: Competitive Training 1 (10 minutes)

sports-graphics.com

Goal of the Exercise

O   Goal shot training with a passive defender

Setup

O   Positon one attacker and one defender in front of the goal.

O   Position the players in front of them.

6

Sequence

O   The player passes to the attacker, who leaves the opponent with a countermovement.

O   The defender only passively defends.

O   The attacker takes the ball in the direction of the goal and shoots at the goal.

Exercise 8: Competitive Training 2 (20 minutes)

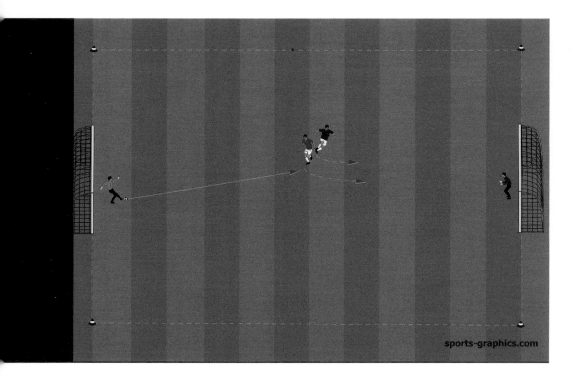

sports-graphics.com

Goal of the Exercise

O   Search for quick goal shots with opponent pressure

Setup

O   Set up a small field with two goals and two goalies.

O   One attacker and one defender are in the small field.

Sequence

O   The goalie passes to the attacker who tries to score a goal in a 1-v-1 against the defender.

O   If the defender gets the ball, he or she can score a goal directly on the opposite side.

O   Every player should act as the attacker and the defender several times.

O   This exercise is very intensive and needs many breaks.

MY FIFTEEN POWER COACHING TIPS FOR THE GOAL SHOT TRAINING

○ **Full Instep:** Run straight to the ball.

○ **Full Instep:** Set the supporting leg next to the ball with the tip of the foot pointing in the shooting direction.

○ **Full Instep:** Stretch out, fixate, and swing the ankle of the shooting leg.

○ **Dropkick:** Like the instep shot, but let the ball quickly jump up next to the foot and then immediately shoot with the instep.

○ **Dropkick:** Depending on the timing of the impact of the ball, the height of the shot can be varied.

○ **Outer Instep:** Run straight or slightly at an angle to the ball.

○ **Outer Instep:** The tip of the foot points down and turns slightly inward.

○ **Outer Instep:** Slightly lean the upper body over the ball.

○ **Outer Instep:** Hit the ball with the outer side of the instep.

○ **Hip Shot:** Take the upper body opposite of the shooting direction. Then heavily tilt to the side over the supporting leg.

○ **Hip Shot:** Horizontally swing the shooting leg almost to the ball.

6

○ **Hip Shot:** Hit the ball with a stretched out and fixed full instep.

○ **Inner Instep:** Run diagonally in the shooting direction.

○ **Inner Instep:** Place the supporting leg sideways behind the ball.

○ **Inner Instep:** Stretch the ankle of the supporting leg, slightly turn it outward, and fixate; hit with the inner instep and follow through with the leg.

HEAD BALL TRAINING

How you can teach your kids how to head and with what exercises can your players immensely improve themselves when performing headers?

The head ball game is only rarely trained these days. However, the head ball game is often used in games with long punts, after a flank, with standard situations, or the respective header defense. The head ball training is strongly neglected as measured by the frequency of its use in match-winning situations.

The prerequisites for a successful header are the timing of the ball, the correct calculation of the trajectory of the ball, and the right moment of the jump.

There are different techniques of the head ball game like the straight header, the header with a change in direction, and the diving header.

A jump with both legs to the header is recommended for the first steps into the head ball game. The next step would be a jump with one leg to the header. The advantage of the jump with one foot is a higher jumping height; the running speed is transferred through the swinging leg movement.

Particularly in the beginning, the coach should make sure that the players have their eyes open during a header. A lighter ball can be used at first to reduce the players' fear.

EIGHT METHODICAL WAYS TO TEACH THE HEAD BALL GAME

O   Pre-exercises for the head ball game

O   Straight header from a standing jump

O   Header from a standing jump with a change in direction

O   Header from a jump with both legs

O   Header after a jump with one leg

O   Header after a jump with one leg with twist

O   Head ball game competitive training

O   Head ball game competitive training

6

Exercise 1: Pre-Exercises for the Head Ball Game (2 minutes)

Goal of the Exercise

O   Feel for the correct hitting spot for headers

Setup

O   Every player gets one ball.

Sequence

O   The player throws the ball up, hits the ball once with his head, and then catches the ball.

O   Further Exercises

O   Juggle a balloon with the head.

O   Place the ball on the forehead and balance as long as possible.

O   Throw the ball up and juggle it as long as possible with the head.

Exercise 2: Straight Header From a Standing Jump (7 minutes)

Goal of the Exercise

O   Straight header from a standing jump

Setup

O   Divide players into two teams.

O   Place two goals next to each other with a goalie in each.

O   Play the balls to the goalie.

Sequence

O   The goalies throw the ball to the first player for a header.

O   The players shoot the ball as a header to the goal from a standing jump.

O   The goalies try to catch the balls.

O   Which team scores more goals?

6

Tips

O   Bring the chin to the chest with a fixed neck.

O   Run forward out of the arch and hit the center of the ball with the forehead.

O   Keep the eyes open!

Exercise 3: Header From a Standing Jump With Change in Direction (5 minutes)

www.sports-graphics.com

Goal of the Exercise
O   Header from a standing jump with a change in direction

Setup
O   Place three cone goals in a triangle formation.
O   Divide players into groups of three.
O   Each player stands in a cone goal.

Sequence
O   Player 1 throws the ball to player 2.
O   Player 2 heads the ball to player 3.
O   Player 3 throws the ball to player 1.
O   Player 1 heads the ball to player two, and so on.
O   Make the exercise more difficult by having the players try to score a goal into one
     of the cone goals.
O   Which player scores the most head ball goals?

Tip
O   Turn the head and upper body into the shooting direction when heading the ball.

Exercise 4: Header From a Jump With Both Legs (10 minutes)

www.sports-graphics.com

Goal of the Exercise

O   Header from a jump with both legs

O   Timing the header

Setup

O   Place two goals across from each other with one goalie in each.

O   Divide players into two teams.

O   Position players on both of the goal.

O   Place the other players centrally behind one another in front of the goal.

Sequence

O   The first player next to the goal throws to the first central player.

O   The player in front of the goal tries to score a head ball goal.

O   Change position and tasks.

O   Which team scored the most head ball goals?

6

Tips

O   Face the ball, gain momentum with the arms, and jump upward, not forward.

O   Bring the chin to the chest with a fixed neck.

O   Run forward out of the arch and hit the center of the ball with the forehead

O   Keep the eyes open!

Exercise 5: Header After a Jump With One Leg (10 minutes)

Goal of the Exercise
○ Header after a jump with one leg
○ Timing of the head ball
○ Header accuracy

Setup
○ Place two goals with goalies across from each other.
○ Mark a jumping line about 16-23 feet in front of the goal.
○ Divide players into two teams.
○ Direct the players to their positions (see figure).

Sequence

O The first player in front of the goal starts running and gets the ball thrown to him from the first player next to the goal.

O The player heads the ball towards the goal after a jump with one leg on the jumping line.

O Change position and task.

O Which team scores more goals?

Tips

O Jump with one leg after a short start-up, and swing the other leg up from the front.

O Swing the jumping leg to gain height and not width.

O Hit the ball at the highest point of the jumping phase.

O Bring the chin to the chest with a fixed neck.

O Run forward out of the arch and hit the center of the ball with the forehead.

6

Exercise 6: Header After a Jump With One Leg With Twist

sports-graphics.com

Goal of the Exercise

O   Header after a jump with one leg

O   Timing of the head ball

O   Header accuracy

Setup

O   Place two goals next to each other with goalies.

O   Place a cone about 16-23 feet in front of the goal.

O   Divide players into two teams.

O   Direct the players to their positions (see figure).

Sequence

- The first player in front of the goal runs around the cone in the direction of the center.
- The player next to the goal throws the ball to the oncoming player in the middle.
- The player in front of the goal shoots at the goal with a header.
- Change position and task.
- Which team scores the most goals?

Tips

- Jump with the leg closest to the ball.
- Pull up the swinging leg into the direction of the ball.
- After jumping, head the ball at highest jumping point.
- Turn the head and upper body into the direction of the shot when heading the ball.

Exercise 7: Head Ball Game Competitive Training: Attackers in Superior Numbers (15 minutes)

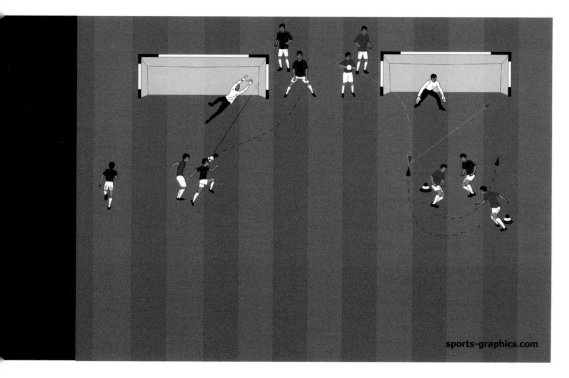

Goal of the Exercise

O   Competitive head ball training in a simplified form

Setup

O   Place two goals next to each other with goalies.

O   Divide players into two teams.

O   Direct the players to their positions (see figure).

Sequence

O   Both attackers in front of the goal coordinate a run towards the goal.

O   The player next to the goal throws the ball to one of the two attackers.

O   The attacker performs the header.

O   The defender tries to fend the ball.

Tips

- O Watch running paths: one to the short post and one to the long post.
- O Build in crosses or running feints to escape the defender.
- O Observe physical exertion in a header duel with the defender.

6

Exercise 8: Competitive Head Ball Training (20-25 minutes)

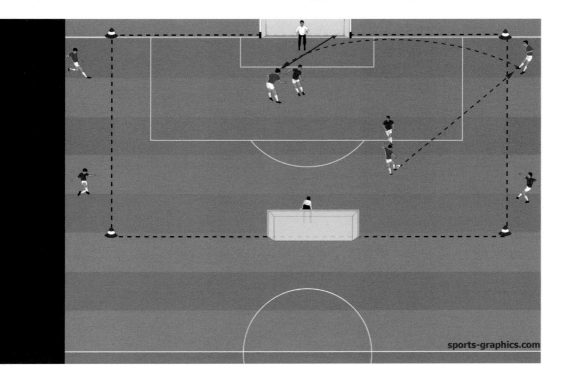

Goal of the Exercise

- O Competitive head ball training
- O Header duels
- O Running paths (one short, one long post, crossing, running feints)
- O Quick switching

Setup

- O Mark a tight playing field between two goals with goalies.
- O Divide players into two teams.
- O Direct the players to their positions (see figure).

Sequence

○   Players play 2-v-2 in a tight playing field.

○   Goals may only be scored with headers after flanks.

○   The passers are not allowed to be hindered while flanking.

○   The passers flank to their players in their team.

○   Exchange the flanker after 5 minutes of playing time.

○   Which team scores the most goals?

6

MY TEN COACHING TECHNIQUE TIPS
FOR HEADER TECHNIQUES!

Straight Header

O   Face the ball, swing the arms, and jump up, not forward.

O   Bring the chin to the chest with a fixed neck.

O   Run forward out of the arch and hit the center of the ball with the forehead.

O   Keep the eyes open!

Header With Change in Direction

O   Jump with the leg closest to the ball, and pull the swinging leg up in the direction
    of the ball.

O   Perform the header at the highest jumping point possible.

O   Rotate the head and upper body into the shooting direction when heading the ball.

Diving Header

O   Hit the ball with the head at hip height to knee height.

O   Jump forward with a lowered upper body and the chin tucked in to the neck.

O   Look at the ball and absorb the landing with your arms stretched out forwards.

FAST STRENGTH TRAINING WITH GOAL SHOTS

This is how you can be that crucial bit faster with successfully shoot a goal!

In many situations, it is important that players have a certain speed with or without the
ball to get around their opponents. The first few yards in particular can be crucial to
winning or losing the game.

Is it possible to improve the acceleration and sprint of a player? Yes, you can improve the
speed of every single one of your players. Through specific exercises and training, your
players will also improve their entire motion process with coordinated speed and will be
that crucial bit faster than the opponent.

Exercise 1: Fast Strength Training

sports-graphics.com

Setup

○ Place five hurdles in a row in front of the penalty area.

○ Place a ball after the last hurdle.

Sequence

○ Players jump over the hurdles without a step in between.

○ Players then dribble the ball up to the penalty area and shoot at the goal.

6

Exercise 2: Fast Strength Training With Goal Shot

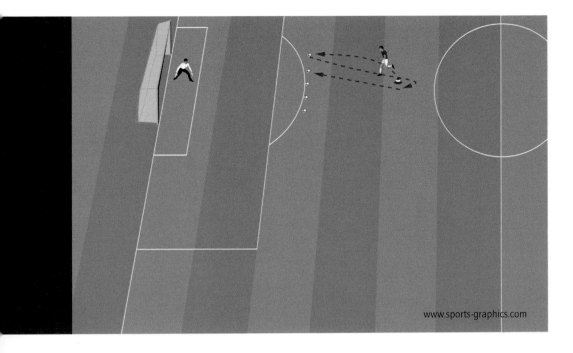

www.sports-graphics.com

Setup

O   Place five balls next to each other about 60 feet in front of the goal.

O   Place a cone about 80 feet in front of the goal.

Sequence

O   The player starts from the cone, sprints to the ball, and shoots at the goal.

O   After the shot, the player sprints directly back to the cone and then to the next ball and shoots at the goal. This pattern continues until all five balls are shot to the goal.

O   Shoot all five ball at the highest speed possible.

O   Who scored the most goals?

Exercise 3: Fast Strength Training With Goal Shot

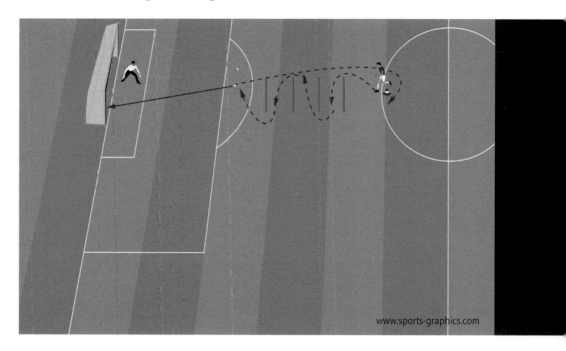

www.sports-graphics.com

Setup

○ Place five poles in a row in front of the penalty area.

○ Place two balls about 60 feet in front of the goal.

Sequence

○ Players run around the poles with quick side steps in a slalom style and then shoot the first ball to the goal.

6

○ They sprint back and do the same again, shooting the second ball towards the goal with the weak leg.

Exercise 4: Fast Strength Training With Goal Shot

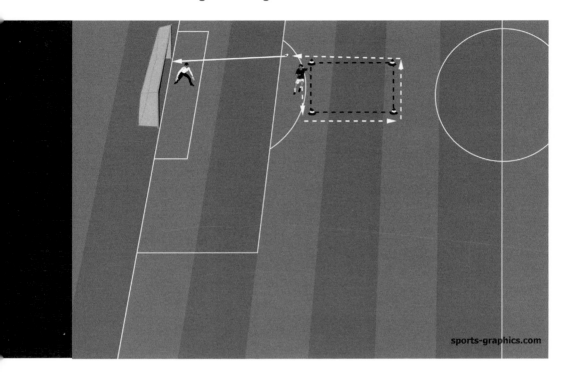

sports-graphics.com

Setup
○   Mark a 16-by-16-foot field in front of the penalty area.
○   Place a ball in front of the penalty area.

Sequence
○   The exercise is always performed with the view on the goal and the highest speed possible.
○   The player starts on the side where the ball is placed.
○   The player goes from the first cone to the second cone with fast side steps.
○   From the second cone to the third cone, the player uses a fast backward run.
○   From the third cone to the fourth cone, the player uses fast side steps again.
○   From the fourth cone, the player sprints to the ball and takes a shot on goal.

THESE MOVES CAN CRACK ANY DEFENSE!

These success-promising moves build a determined and quick attacking game. If you consequently train these moves with your team over and over again, these game structures will become a habit and your players will be ahead of their opponents.

A team needs organization and a lot of training to crack an opponent's defense. As the coach, you must put together training exercises that will allow your team to outplay the opposing team.

Soccer: The 6-Week Plan

Exercise 1: Training Tip With First Move

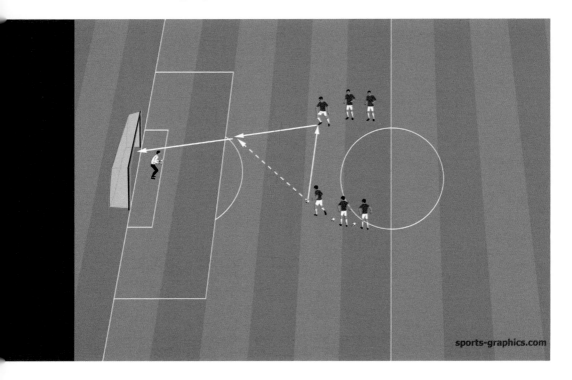

sports-graphics.com

Setup
O Place two dolls or poles about 80 feet in front of the goals as defensive players.
O This exercise uses only half of the field.

Sequence
O Player 1 passes the ball to player 2 and runs into the depth behind the defense.
O Player 2 takes the ball and passes it by the dolls on the right side into the depth.
O Player 1 takes the ball and shoots at the goal.
O Make sure that player 1 does not stand offsides during the pass from player 2.

Exercise 2: Training Tip With Second Moves

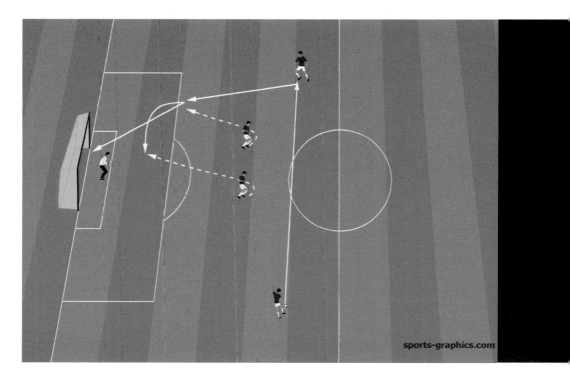

Setup

O Place two dolls or poles about 80 feet in front of the goals as defensive players.

O This exercise uses only half of the field.

Sequence

O Player 1 passes to player 2.

O While player 2 takes the ball, player 3 quickly comes forward, turns away in a flash, and sprints into the depth.

O Player 2 passes the ball into the run of player 3, who then shoots the ball towards the goal.

O Player 4 runs after and waits for a rebound from the goalie or for a cross pass.

O Make sure there is no offside during the pass from player 2.

Soccer: The 6-Week Plan

Exercise 3: Training Tip With Third Moves

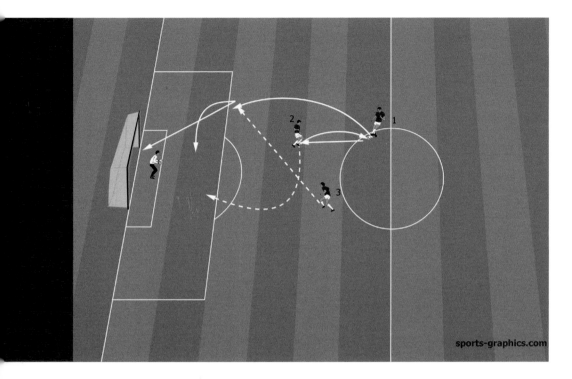

Setup
O   Place two dolls or poles about 80 feet in front of the goals as defensive players.
O   This exercise uses only half of the field.

Sequence
O   Player 2 comes forward quickly, while player 1 passes the ball to player 2.
O   Player 2 lets the ball bump to player 1 and turns to create free space as player 3 runs diagonally into the depth.
O   Player 1 passes the ball into the depth, where player 3 runs in.
O   Player 2 runs to the front.
O   Player 3 shoots towards the goal or passes to player 2.

Exercise 4: Training Tip With Three Moves

sports-graphics.com

Setup

O   Place three dolls or poles as defending players in front of the penalty area.

O   This exercise uses only half of the field.

Sequence

6

O   Player 1 passes to player 2 who comes foward quickly, feints taking the ball, and lets it roll to player 3.

O   Player 2 cancels the feint and runs into the depth.

O   At the same time, player 3 passes the ball directly into the free space to player 2.

O   Player 2 shoots at the goal.

Toto Schmugge Trainings: Tip 1

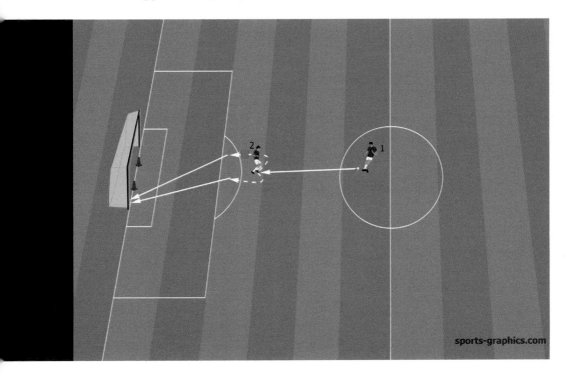

Goal

O   Shooting accuracy

Setup

O   Place a cone about 5 feet next to the goal post on both sides.

O   Place a cone about 80 feet away from the goal and centered in front of it.

O   One attacker stands at the cone with a passer in front.

Sequence

O   Player 1 passes to player 2.

O   Player 2 takes the ball to the right or left and runs to the goal.

O   Player 2 shoots into the goal either from the right or left.

Toto Schmugge Trainings: Tip 2

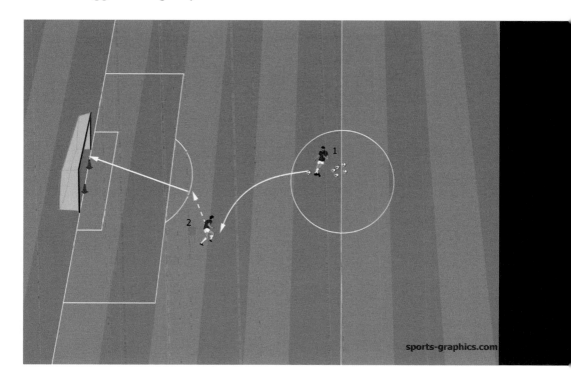

Goal
- O   Shooting accuracy
- O   Receiving and taking ball

Setup
- O   Place a cone about 5 feet next to the goal post on both sides.
- O   Place a cone about 80 feet away and slightly to the side of the goal.
- O   Assign one passer to the half field and one attacker in front of the goal.

Sequence
- O   Player 1 plays a long volley to player 2.
- O   Player 2 takes the ball while running and tries to hit the goal left or right in front of the penalty area.

6

Soccer: The 6-Week Plan

Toto Schmugge Trainings: Trainings: Tip 3

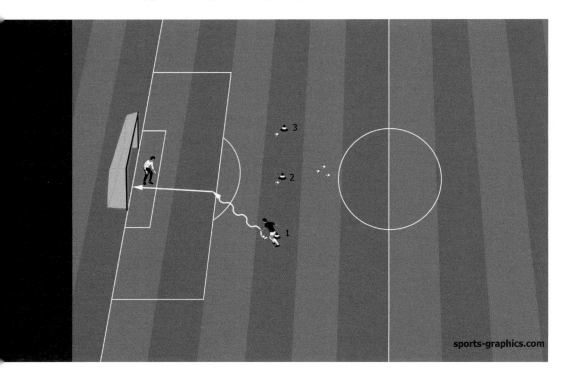

Goal

O   Shooting accuracy

Setup

O   Position three cones spread out around the penalty area.

O   Set up one goal with a goalie.

Sequence

O   The attacker dribbles alone from different positions towards the goalie and tries to play him out or shoot a goal directly.

Exercise 1: Goal Shot Speed

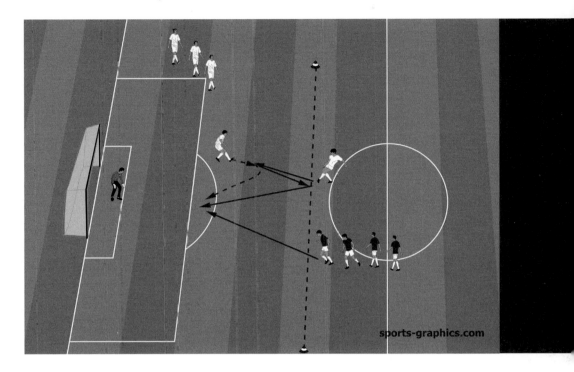

sports-graphics.com

Setup
O   Mark a line about 100-130 feet in front of the goal.
O   Defenders position themselves on the line.
O   The coach stands on the marked line with a supply of balls.

Sequence
O   The attacker claims the ball from the coach about 30 feet in front with acceleration and the coach passes the ball to the player.
O   The attacker lets the ball bump to the coach and sprints in the direction of the goal.
O   The coach plays the ball to the player while he or she is running.
O   Meanwhile, the defending player sprints from the marked line to hinder the attacker's shot on goal.
O   Switch tasks and perform the exercise from different positions.
O   Which group scored more goals?

6

Exercise 2: Goal Shot Speed

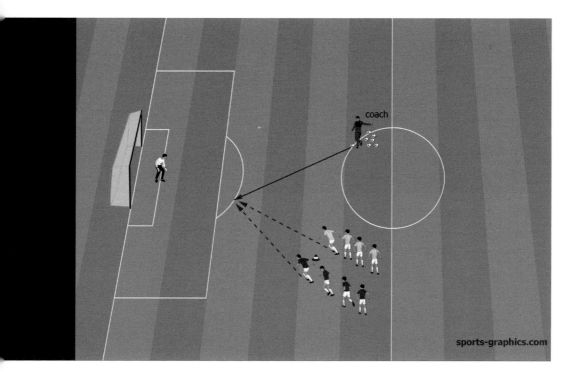

Setup

- O   This exercise uses only half of the field.
- O   Place a cone about 80 feet from the baseline.
- O   Divide the players into teams of two.
- O   Position the attackers on the outer side and about 3 feet closer to the goal while the defenders stand on the inner side about 3 feet meter behind them.
- O   The coach stands slightly offset and behind with the balls.

Sequence

- O   The coach plays different balls (e.g., flat, bouncing, half high) into the field in the direction of the goal.
- O   The attacker tries to score a goal against the defender.
- O   The defender tries to hinder the goal shot.
- O   Have players switch positions.
- O   Which player shot the most goals?

Exercise 3: Goal Shot Speed

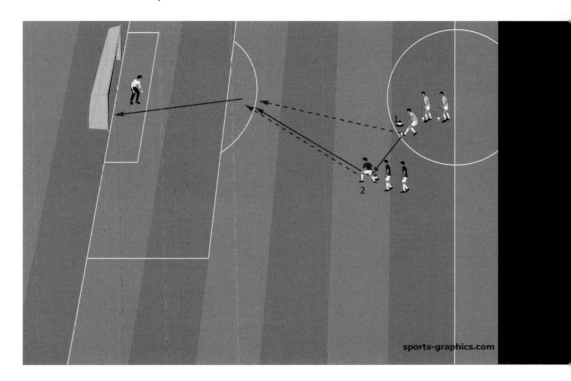

Setup

O   This exercise uses only half of the field.

O   Mark a cone goal for the attackers on the side about 100 feet in front of the goal.

O   Mark a cone in the middle about 80 feet in front of the goal for the defenders.

O   Divide the players into teams of two.

O   Each team gets a ball.

6

Sequence

O   Player 1 passes to player 2 and runs into the depth.

O   Player 2 passes the ball directly into the depth and sprints after it.

O   Player 1 tries to score a goal.

O   Player 2 tries to hinder the goal.

O   Players switch positions.

O   Which player scored the most goals?

FOUR IMPORTANT EXERCISES
FOR SUCCESSFUL GOAL SHOT TRAINING!

When shooting at the goal, not only does the goal shot have to fit but also the movement process and the technique before even coming to a goal shot.

I have put together exercises for you that allow players to perform goal shot exercises with movement processes in the training. However, remember that passing games have to be learned too. If players cannot play a concentrated pass, the team will not be able to score a goal because the pass does not arrive.

You should perform the goal shot training on two goals to prevent long waiting times for your players. You should also perform a goal shot competition, which forces players to be more focused because every team wants to win.

Exercise 1: Goal Shot

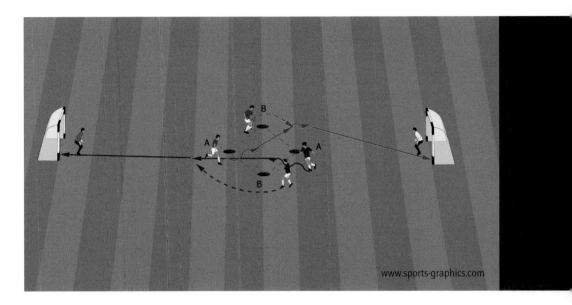

www.sports-graphics.com

Setup

O   Place two goals about 130-160 feet apart.

O   Use four cones to mark a 32-by-32-foot square in the middle of the field with four cones (see figure).

O   Divide players into two groups.

Sequence

6

O   Two players (As) dribble from the cone that's close to the goal to each other.

O   The players quickly dribble in front of one another, do a feint, and dribble past each other.

O   The other two players (Bs) start with a running feint around the cone and run into the depth.

O   The players (As) pass the ball to players (B) into the run.

O   Player B shoots at the goal from a full run.

O   Player A positions himself at the starting position of player B, and player B positions himself at the starting position of player A.

O   The group that scores the most goals is the winner.

O   The losing group must do an exercise as a penalty (e.g., 10-20 push-ups).

Exercise 2: Goal Shot

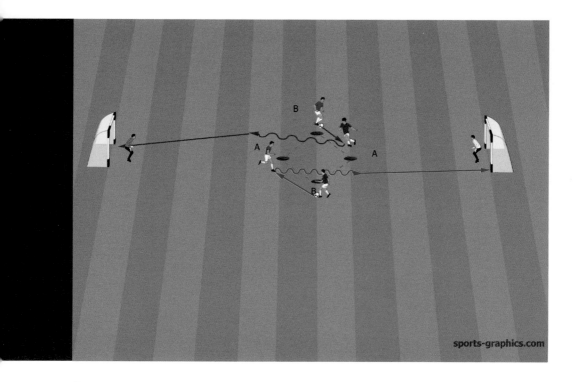

sports-graphics.com

Setup

O   Place two goals about 130-160 feet apart.

O   Use four cones to mark a 32-by-32-foot square in the middle of the field (see figure).

O   Divide players into two groups.

Sequence

O   Player B passes to player A.

O   Player A takes the ball and does a feint in front of the opponent.

O   After the feint, player A shoots at the goal.

O   Player A then positions himself at the starting position of player B, and player B positions himself at the starting position of player A.

O   The group that scores the most goals wins.

O   The losing group must do an exercise as a penalty (e.g., 10-20 push-ups).

Exercise 3: Goal Shot

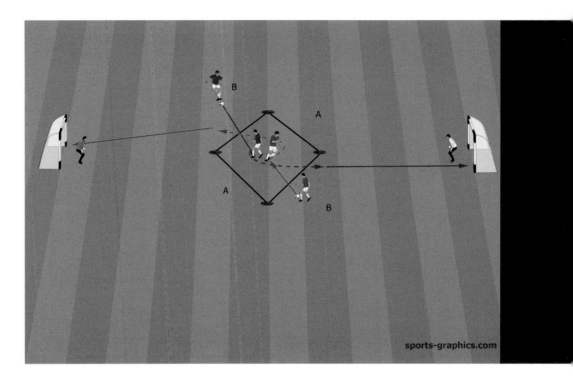

sports-graphics.com

Setup

O   Place two goals about 130-160 feet apart.

O   Use four cones to mark a 32-by-32-foot square in the middle of the field (see figure).

O   Divide players into two groups.

Sequence

6

O   Player B passes to player A.

O   Player A takes the ball and dribbles around the opponent to the cone and does a feint in front of the cone.

O   After the feint, player A takes a shot on goal.

O   Player A then positions himself at the starting position of player B, and player B positions himself at the starting position of player A.

O   The group that scores the most goals wins.

O   The losing group must do an exercise as a penalty (e.g., 10-20 push-ups).

Exercise 4: Goal Shot

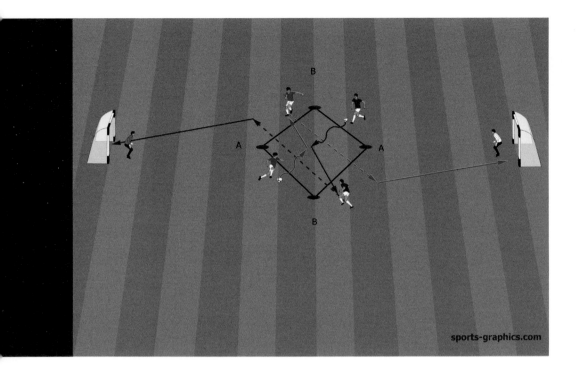

Setup

O   Place two goals about 130-160 feet apart.

O   Use four cones to mark a 32-by-32-foot square in the middle of the field (see figure).

O   Divide players into two groups.

Sequence

O   Both A players dribble the ball towards each other and then pass to player B.

O   Player A sprints into the depth.

O   Player B directly plays a double pass into the run of player A.

O   Player A shoots at the goal from a full run.

O   Player A then positions himself at the starting position of player B, and player B positions himself at the starting position of player A.

O   The group that scores the most goals wins.

O   The losing group must do an exercise as a penalty (e.g., 10-20 push-ups).

THREE EXCITING EXERCISES
FOR SUCCESSFUL SCISSOR TRAINING!

Your players will be even more unpredictable with this! Every player should dominate a scissor. The more perfect a player can do a scissor, the more unpredictable they are to their opponents.

With a scissor, the player can individually outplay his opponent. Nowadays, there are fewer and fewer street soccer players. Your task as a coach is to teach or improve your players' skills and techniques.

Exercise 1: Goal Shot With a Scissor

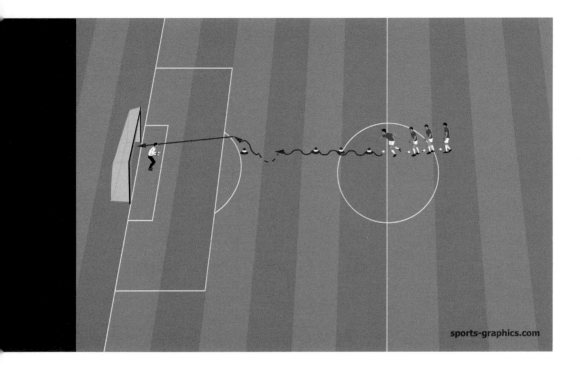

sports-graphics.com

Setup

O   Place three cones in a row about 30 feet in front of the penalty area.

O   Place another cone about 15 feet in front of the penalty area.

O   Each player gets a ball.

Sequence

O   Players dribble around the cones in a slalom.

O   At the penalty area in front of the cone, the cone is played out with a scissor.

O   Players then shoot at the goal.

Exercise 2: Goal Shot With a Scissor

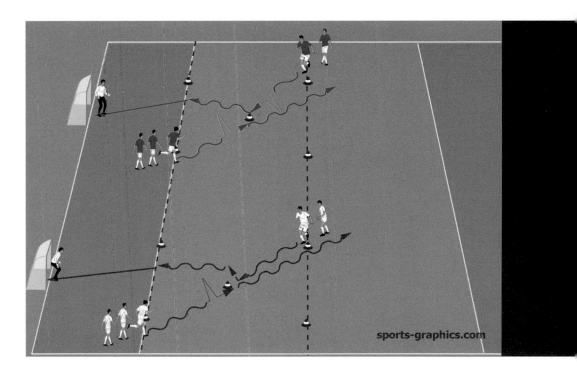

Setup

O   Place two goals on the baseline.

O   Mark two 20-by-10-foot fields about 60 feet in front of the goals.

O   Mark the middle of the field with a cone.

O   Divide players into two teams.

O   The players of each team stand diagonally across from each other in the field.

O   Each player has a ball.

6

Sequence

O   Two players of a group dribble diagonally towards the cone in the middle and do a scissor in front of the cone.

O   The player who runs toward the goal shoots at the goal while the other player queues up for a goal shot.

O   Which team scores the most goals?

Soccer: The 6-Week Plan

Exercise 3: Goal Shot With a Scissor

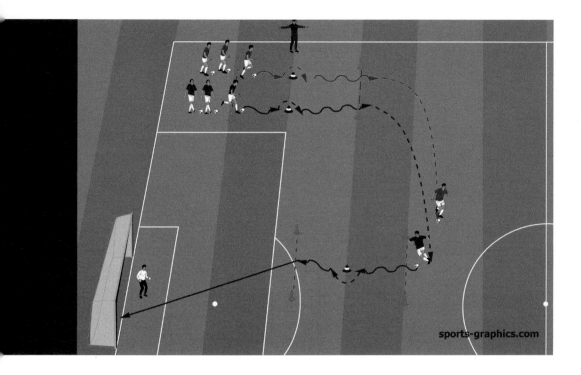

sports-graphics.com

Setup

O   Mark two courses next to the goal by placing three cones 20 feet away from each
     other.

O   Mark a field in front of the penalty area and place a cone in the middle.

O   Divide players into two teams.

Sequence

O   Players dribble through the course next to the penalty area.

O   Players do a scissor in front of the cone in the middle.

O   Players dribble to the field and do a scissor again in front of the cone in the middle.

O   After the scissor, players shoot towards the goal.

O   Which team scores more goals?

6

Week 1
_____

Week 2
_____

Week 3
_____

Week 4
_____

Week 5
_____

Week 6
_____

CREDITS

Cover design: Sannah Inderelst

Cover photo: Thinkstock®

Inside layout: Sannah Inderelst

Illustrations: Toto Schmugge

Typesetting: www.satzstudio-hilger.de

Copyediting: Anne Rumery, Kristina Oltrogge